Lime**r**ick C...

KU-284-681

30012 **00615457** 8

DK EYEWITNESS TOP 10 TRAVEL GUIDES

VIRGIN ISLANDS

LYNDA LOHR

917·2

Left **Village Marina Cay, Tortola** Right **View from Fort Christiansvaern, St. Croix**

LONDON, NEW YORK,
MELBOURNE, MUNICH AND DELHI
www.dk.com

Produced by Dorling Kindersley
India Pvt Ltd, New Delhi

Reproduced by Colourscan, Singapore
Printed and bound in Italy by Graphicom

First published in Great Britain in 2004
by Dorling Kindersley Limited
80 Strand, London WC2R 0RL
A Penguin Company

Copyright 2004 ©
Dorling Kindersley Limited, London

All rights reserved. No part of this publication
may be reproduced, stored in a retrieval system,
or transmitted in any form or by any means,
electronic, mechanical, photocopying, recording
or otherwise, without the prior written permission
of the copyright owner.

A CIP catalogue record is available from
the British Library.

ISBN 1-4053-0333-6

Within each Top 10 list in this book, no
hierarchy of quality or popularity is implied.
All 10 are, in the editor's opinion, of
roughly equal merit.

Contents

Virgin Islands' Top 10

The information in this
DK Eyewitness Top 10 Travel Guide is checked regularly.
Every effort has been made to ensure that this book is as up-to-date as possible at the
time of going to press. Some details, however, such as telephone numbers, opening hours,
prices, gallery hanging arrangements and travel information are liable to change.
The publishers cannot accept responsibility for any consequences arising from the use
of this book, nor for any material on third party websites, and cannot guarantee that any
website address in this book will be a suitable source of travel information. We value
the views and suggestions of our readers very highly. Please write to:
Publisher, DK Eyewitness Travel Guides,
Dorling Kindersley, 80 Strand, London WC2R 0RL, Great Britain.

Left **Marine Gardens, Coral World, St. Thomas** Right **View from Drake's Seat, St. Thomas**

Left **Sailing in North Sound, Virgin Gorda** Right **Leaning palm trees on Carambola Beach, St Croix**

Key to abbreviations
USVI *US Virgin Islands* **BVI** *British Virgin Islands* **Adm** *admission charge payable*

3

VIRGIN ISLANDS' TOP 10

VIRGIN ISLANDS' TOP 10

🔟 Highlights of the Virgin Islands

Mere specks in the Caribbean, the US and British Virgin Islands sit within eyesight of each other. The Stars and Stripes flutters over St. Croix, St. John, and St. Thomas and the Union Jack over Tortola, Virgin Gorda, and the outer islands, but all offer tropical sun, soft sand beaches, and turquoise sea. In both territories motorists drive on the left, a decidedly British practice, while the US dollar serves as legal tender. However, each island has its own ambience, from the bustle in St. Thomas to downright sleepiness in the outer BVIs.

1 Historic St. Croix

First settled in 1625 by Holland and England, with other European countries following, this former Danish colony reveals its history at every turn of the road. The Danish influence is especially obvious in the island's two main towns, Christiansted and Frederiksted *(see pp8–9)*.

Jost Van Dyke

St. Thomas

Charlotte Amalie **4** **5**   **6**   Cruz Bay

U.S. VIRGIN ISLANDS

3

2

St. John

Caribbean Sea

3 Stroll Through Cruz Bay, St. John

Tucked next to a pretty harbor, this cozy town stretches inland for several blocks. It offers eclectic shops, bars, restaurants, and people-watching within walking distance *(see pp12–13)*.

2 Virgin Islands National Park, St. John

Established in 1956, this park occupies about two-thirds of this 20-sq mile (52-sq km) island. Besides a range of plants and animals, it features gorgeous beaches, hiking trails on its lush hillsides, interesting ruins along the hills and coasts, and water-sports galore *(see pp10–11)*.

4 Duty-free Shopping in St. Thomas

Good prices, thanks to a duty-free deal from the US government, and the variety of merchandise make this a shopping mecca *(see pp14–15)*.

St. Croix

1

Christiansted

Frederiksted

Previous pages **Fruit and catch of the day at a beach in St. Thomas**

Anegada

5 Historic Charlotte Amalie, St. Thomas

Settled by Denmark in 1666, this town is the island's historical hub. Streets carry Danish names and many buildings date back several centuries *(see pp16–17)*.

Caribbean Sea

Virgin Gorda

Tortola Spanish Town•

•Road Town

BRITISH VIRGIN ISLANDS

Salt Island *Cooper Island*

8 ⌐———⌐ 4 ⌐ miles ⌐ 0 ⌐ km ⌐ 4 ⌐———⌐ 8

Peter Island

Norman Island

6 Coral World, St. Thomas

This marine park connects visitors with the undersea life around the islands. Watch colorful fish in tanks or up close on underwater adventures such as Sea Trekkin' or Snuba *(see pp18–19)*.

7 BVI National Parks & Scenic Spots

History, hiking, diving, and lovely sea views greet visitors who seek out these special places. Some are off the beaten path, but all are worth the effort *(see pp20–21)*.

8 Sailing in the British Virgin Islands

Year-round balmy weather, gorgeous scenery, and pristine anchorages just a day's sail from each other make this one of the top sailing destinations in the world *(see pp22–3)*.

9 Dive & Snorkel Trips

Reefs teeming with colorful fish and coral provide interesting diving no matter where you go, but the best diving is found offshore on a boat trip *(see pp24–5)*.

10 Beach Resorts

Total calm and laziness by the sea or an abundance of activities – Virgin Islands' top resorts offer everything to make your holiday a dream come true *(see pp26–7)*.

⓰ Historic St. Croix

Once divided into 224 estates, St. Croix has a plantation past that continued long after the end of slavery in 1848, as indicated by its many 18th- and 19th-century great houses and sugar mills. Since 1625, five of the big European colonial powers have raised their flag here. The most influential were the Danish, who ruled from 1733 to 1917, when the island, along with St. Thomas and St. John, became a US territory.

Interior, Whim Plantation Museum

🅒 Except for Christiansted and Frederiksted, you'll need a rental car or taxi tour to see the sights. Make sure you get a free map at your hotel, rental car agency, or the tourism office. Gas stations do not sell maps.

🅡 You'll find a range of restaurants in Christiansted and Frederiksted, but bring lunch or snacks for a picnic. St. George Village Botanical Garden and Whim Plantation Museum make lovely choices.

• Little Princess Estate: D4; Just off Rte 75, turn north at the Five Corners traffic light; 340-773-5575; Open 3–5pm Tue & Thu

• Estate Mount Washington: A5; Off Ham's Bluff Rd (Rte 63), watch for the sign; 340-772-1026; Open dawn–dusk daily

Top 10 Sights

1. Historic Christiansted
2. Christiansted National Historic Site
3. Fort Christianvaern
4. Little Princess Estate
5. Judith's Fancy
6. St. George Village Botanical Garden
7. Whim Plantation Museum
8. Estate Mount Washington
9. Carl & Marie Lawaetz Museum
10. Historic Frederiksted

⓵ Historic Christiansted

Named after the then Danish king, this gracious town's *(right)* construction started in 1735. Centered on the harbor, it has streets running uphill from the waterfront and distinctly 18th-century European architecture *(see p57)*.

⓶ Christiansted National Historic Site

Operated by the National Park Service, this waterfront area features several historic buildings. Apart from Fort Christianvaern, there are the Scale House where sugar was weighed, Customs House, and Post Office. The Steeple Building *(right)* has a small museum *(see p57)*.

⓷ Fort Christianvaern

The centerpiece of the Christiansted National Historic Site, this imposing yellow edifice at the water's edge dates to 1749. Its dungeons, ramparts, and cannons *(above)* provide interesting exploring. Park rangers answer questions and offer tours *(see p57)*.

⓸ Little Princess Estate

Now in the midst of restoration, this 24-acre 19th-century plantation is run by the international group, The Nature Conservancy. An easy stroll takes you past ruins of the windmill, the sugar and rum factory, the laborers' village, and the gardens where the many native and exotic plants are labeled.

Judith's Fancy

5 The remains of a great house and tower sit in the heart of this posh neighborhood, named after the woman buried near the ruins. Christopher Columbus halted at nearby Salt River Bay in 1493 (see p40).

St. George Village Botanical Garden

6 Around 1,500 varieties of leafy plants and flowers surround the ruins of a 19th-century sugar plantation village. Its gardens (right) include examples of each of St. Croix's ecosystems ranging from an arid cactus garden to a lush rainforest (see p58).

Whim Plantation Museum

7 Restored by the St. Croix Landmarks Society, this estate boasts a fine 18th-century great house. The oval-shaped mansion is filled with antiques, including a four-poster bed and old photos of St. Croix. Outbuildings include a kitchen, sugar factory, and windmill (see p58).

Carl & Marie Lawaetz Museum

9 This circa 1750 gem was the home of the prominent Lawaetz family. Often, a Lawaetz family member conducts tours that include stops at the four-poster mahogany bed (left) shared by Carl and Marie, the dining room with its hand-painted china, and the gardens that fed the family for generations (see p58).

Estate Mount Washington

8 The extensive stone ruins of this old sugar plantation include a mill and a rum factory. The ruins were discovered underneath foliage by the owners of the adjacent house.

Historic Frederiksted

10 Charming Frederiksted dates to 1751 (see p58). Fort Frederik, near the cruise ship pier, is the town's historical focus. Here, freedom was granted to the island's slaves on July 3, 1848 (see p48).

Check out antiques at the shop that operates next to the ruins at Estate Mount Washington

🔟 Virgin Islands National Park, St. John

Green mountains meet white, sandy shores at this showcase of the National Park Service, which occupies two-thirds of St. John's area. A mix of native and introduced species thrive among its varied vegetation, which ranges from moist subtropical forests to semi-arid scrublands. The park's inhabitants include gecko and iguana lizards, sea turtles, bats, reef fish, and more than 30 species of tropical birds. Visitors can swim, snorkel, and scuba-dive pristine reefs, or hike past stone ruins left from the days of sugar and slavery.

View from North Shore Road

🕐 The park's beaches are open 24 hours, but for safety's sake, limit your visit to daylight hours. Explore the park during the cooler morning or late afternoon hours. The midday tropical sun burns bright at this latitude.

🍽 While you'll find restaurants in Cruz Bay and Coral Bay, options inside the park are limited to pricey restaurants at Caneel Bay Resort and more pedestrian ones at Cinnamon Bay Campground and Maho Bay Camps. Trunk Bay has a snack bar that sells burgers. Bring your lunch or snacks for a picnic under the palm trees.

- Map E2
- VINP Visitor's Center: Map D2; Rte 20 at the Creek, Cruz Bay; 340-776-6201; www.nps.gov/viis; Open 8am–4:30pm daily

Top 10 Sights

1. Virgin Islands National Park Visitor's Center
2. Salomon Beach
3. North Shore Road (Route 20)
4. Hawksnest Bay
5. Trunk Bay Beach
6. Annaberg Plantation
7. Salt Pond Bay
8. Lameshur Bay & Beach
9. Reef Bay Hike
10. Explore the Nooks & Crannies in a Kayak

1 Virgin Islands National Park Visitor's Center

Start your visit to the park here *(below)*. Rangers are on hand with maps and brochures, and advice on how best to use your time. Displays explain the park's natural and cultural history. A small store sells books and gift items.

2 Salomon Beach

Hike downhill from behind the Visitor's Center for 20 minutes to the only beach within walking distance of Cruz Bay. Worth the effort for a few hours at the soft, sandy beach or snorkeling the nearby rocks and reefs. 🔎 *Map D2*

3 North Shore Road (Route 20)

Don't miss a drive along this gorgeous route. Overlooks let motorists safely view the spectacular sea and mountain vistas *(see p40)*. Pick up a map at the Visitor's Center before setting out. 🔎 *Map D2*

➡ The park and tour operators offer organized trips, but you can easily strike out on your own

Hawksnest Bay
4 Seagrapes and palm trees fringe this stunning strand of sand. Snorkel the patchy reefs that sit just offshore, stroll along the water's edge, or simply while away hours on your beach towel. Facilities include basic toilets, a changing room, and simple pavilions *(see p63)*.

Trunk Bay Beach
5 The park's busiest beach, Trunk Bay *(left)* features an underwater snorkel trail with signs to explain the sights. It's popular with cruise ship tours, so come early or late for solitude *(see p63)*.

Annaberg Plantation
6 A huge stone windmill *(right)* is the centerpiece of this restored 18th-century sugar plantation, which includes a sugar factory, a tiny jail, and the remains of a slave village. Ranger talks here highlight the island's agrarian past *(see p64)*.

Lameshur Bay & Beach
8 It's a bit of a drive to Lameshur on a mostly paved road, but it's worth the trip if you crave a sparsely populated beach. The snorkeling, particularly on the east side of the bay, is superb, while the ruins in the west are fun to explore. An outhouse provides the only facilities. Map E2

Salt Pond Bay
7 Sun or snorkel at this sandy beach, or, for some adventure, hike up Ram's Head for its fine views *(above)*. Follow the signs on the beach's south side. The only facilities here are an outhouse and picnic tables. Map F2

Explore the Nooks & Crannies in a Kayak
10 Rent kayaks at Cinnamon Bay Campground or Maho Bay Camps *(see p115)* to explore the park's nautical byways *(left)*. Kayaks are easy to maneuver, and you won't mind a spill because the water is warm. Pull the kayak up on shore to spend time snorkeling.

Reef Bay Hike
9 With park rangers, trek down this trail to the old Reef Bay Estate, past flora, fauna, and a natural pool inscribed with ancient petroglyphs *(above)*. A boat meets hikers for a ride back to Cruz Bay *(see p67)*.

Stroll Through Cruz Bay, St. John

St. John's main town welcomes visitors with a palm-fringed scimitar of white sand that belies the bustle of its streets. With its narrow roads and traffic that moves at a crawl, it is a stroller's paradise. The streets run on a grid inland from the picturesque harbor, and are lined with interesting boutiques, bars, and fine restaurants. Lovely Cruz Bay Park near the waterfront is perfect for people-watching. Necessities such as the bank, the post office, and the tourism office lie within a block or two of each other in this charming tropical town.

Cruz Bay Park

Conch blower statue, Cruz Bay Park

🗿 Cruz Bay can get unpleasantly busy during morning and evening rush hours. If you're driving, avoid the waterfront.

🍽 You'll find restaurants in Mongoose Junction and Wharfside Village shopping centers and throughout Cruz Bay. Outdoor tables adjacent to the VINP Visitor's Center provide a nice picnic spot.

• Map D2
• Battery: Open 8am–5pm Mon–Fri
• Tourism Office: Henry Samuel St; 340-776-6450; Open 8am–5pm Mon–Fri
• Post Office: Henry Samuel St; Open 7:30am–4pm Mon–Fri, 7:30am–noon Sat
• Elaine I. Sprauve Library: Off Rte 104, 340-776-6359; Open 9am–5pm Mon–Fri

Top 10 Sights

1. Ferry Dock
2. Battery
3. Tourism Office
4. Post Office
5. Virgin Islands National Park Visitor's Center
6. Mongoose Junction Shopping Center
7. Elaine I. Sprauve Library
8. Nazareth Lutheran Church
9. Wharfside Village Shopping Center
10. Cruz Bay Park

Ferry Dock
Unless they come by private boat, all visitors arrive via ferry at the public dock next to a stretch of beach where smaller boats are moored *(below)*. Porters will carry your luggage to the transportation area. A take-out spot just steps away from the dock sells sandwiches, snacks, and drinks.

Battery
Visible from Cruz Bay harbor, the red-roofed Battery was built in 1825 as a courthouse and prison for the island's slaves. The cannons and jail cells remain. It now serves as the local government seat. You can explore the lovely grounds.

Tourism Office
The local government's tourism office sits tucked away in a small park next to the post office. This is the place to go for maps and brochures on places to stay and various activities available in St. John.

4 Post Office
This tiny branch of the US Postal Service is the only place in St. John to mail postcards. While there's a stamp-vending machine in the lobby, it doesn't always work. The lines at the counter can be very long.

5 Virgin Islands National Park Visitor's Center
Stop by here *(right)* for maps, brochures, and information on the latest park activities. The center also features exhibits about the park's history, flora, and fauna *(see p10)*.

6 Mongoose Junction Shopping Center
Built of stone with steps and pathways on several levels, this quaint shopping center *(left)* has an eclectic set of shops and restaurants, as well as a parking lot and public facilities *(see p68)*.

7 Elaine I. Sprauve Library
Named after a dedicated government employee, the library is housed in the 1757 Estate Enighed great house, restored in 1982. It has an interesting collection of locally written books *(below)*.

8 Nazareth Lutheran Church
Dating to 1720, this small church *(below)* is home to one of the island's oldest congregations. Its doors are open during the day – feel free to peep inside. For a glimpse of local life, attend Sunday services.

9 Wharfside Village Shopping Center
Sitting on Cruz Bay Beach, this is an attractive shopping center with flowers fringing its walkways. You'll find a watersports center, several good restaurants, and many shops.

10 Cruz Bay Park
Benches shaded by old trees and attractive gardens beckon strollers to sit for a while in the small park across the street from the waterfront. A statue of a man blowing a conch at the park's edge commemorates the July 3, 1848 emancipation from slavery *(see p48)*.

Cruz Bay Photos, in Wharfside Village Shopping Center, is the only place to get film developed in St. John

TOP 10 Duty-Free Shopping in St. Thomas

A shopper's delight, St. Thomas's duty-free status dates to Danish days, when the Danish government made it a free port. This is what helps lure nearly 1.5 million people to the island each year. You can shop till you drop, or spend only a few hours strolling Charlotte Amalie's old shopping district, or make a quick dash into the nearest mall or hotel gift shop for a bottle of duty-free liquor or a trinket to take back home.

Rum cake

Travelers from the US can take home $1,200 worth of goods from St. Thomas without paying duty. UK travelers may bring home goods of the value of £145 from St. Thomas, along with fixed quantities of liquor, cigarettes, perfume, and eau de toilette. Travelers from other countries should check before they leave home to see how much duty they'll have to pay to shop in the USVI.

• Havensight Mall: Map B2; Havensight Rd (Rte 30)
• Kmart: Map C2; Tutu Park Mall, Rte 38, Tutu; Map B2; Lockhart Plaza, Rte 313, Sugar Estate
• Vendors Plaza: Map P3; Veterans Dr, Charlotte Amalie
• A.H. Riise: Map N2; 37 Main St, Charlotte Amalie

Top 10 Shopping

1. Main Street, Charlotte Amalie
2. Havensight Mall
3. Kmart
4. Vendors Plaza
5. A.H. Riise Department Store
6. The Art Scene
7. Made in the Islands
8. Jewelry
9. Electronics & Cameras
10. Liquor

1 Main Street, Charlotte Amalie

Stores sit cheek-by-jowl along Main Street *(below)* in old stone buildings that once served as warehouses for the sugar trade, providing a delightful ambience for shopping. Interesting bargains, especially for items such as perfume and jewelry, are possible, thanks to the territory's duty-free status. ⚓ *Map N2*

2 Havensight Mall

Sitting next to the cruise ship docks at Havensight, this busy alfresco mall *(above)* caters to cruise ship passengers and shoppers who don't want to brave the crowds filling Main Street, Charlotte Amalie. Many Main Street stores have branches here.

Shopping in Charlotte Amalie

3 Kmart

Shop with the locals at Kmart, a US department store chain, for bathing suits, shorts, t-shirts, beach sandals, sunscreen, and other incidentals at prices much lower than those at hotel gift shops. Its liquor store has a large selection at very reasonable duty-free prices.

If you're shopping for something specific, check prices at home and on the Internet before you land in St. Thomas

5 A.H. Riise Department Store

This venerable store has its roots in the A.H. Riise Pharmacy, which opened in 1840. The only place in the island to sell Rolex watches, this one-stop store carries vast lines of quality goods, including china, crystal, and jewelry *(left)*.

4 Vendors Plaza

Colorful umbrellas shade vendors at this outdoor market across from the Charlotte Amalie waterfront. There's everything from crafts to designer handbags, but watch for knockoffs that carry fake designer labels.

6 The Art Scene

St. Thomas has a huge art scene, with galleries *(below)* scattered around the island and on Main Street. Quality varies, but there are some excellent local artists. Most works have a tropical feel, but occasionally artists depart from the norm.

7 Made in the Islands

Instead of a t-shirt, take home gifts that reflect the Caribbean. Stores all over the islands carry inexpensive jewelry, ceramic pieces, artwork, packaged foods, and more, hand-made by local artisans.

8 Jewelry

St. Thomas's duty-free position usually makes jewelry a bargain. Many stores carry pieces with a variety of gems and worth thousands of dollars, but you can also find less expensive articles. Some jewelry stores will design items to your specifications.

9 Electronics & Cameras

While merchants tout bargain prices on electronics and cameras, you might do better at your hometown discount store. However, you may find models and accessories not easily available. The knowledgeable sales people can help you pick the right equipment.

10 Liquor

Spirits are sold in many different types of stores, including supermarkets, convenience stores, and department stores. While you can buy quality brands of the usual gin and scotch, try a Caribbean liqueur like Coco Lopez or a bottle of St. Croix's Cruzan Rum for a take-home treat *(left)*.

For more shops in St. Thomas **See p78**

🔟 Historic Charlotte Amalie, St. Thomas

At the heart of St. Thomas's history, this city was settled by the Danes in 1666. Its name was changed from Tap Hus (Beer Hall) to honor the wife of Danish King Christian V. Pirates used the city as a hide-out until the mid-18th century, when merchants began to open shops on Main Street. It gained in importance after becoming a free port in 1764 and served as the West Indian sugar trade center until the mid-19th century.

Shuttered window, Seven Arches Museum

🕐 The historic sites are spread out and require some walking. To see them all, you'll need a full day.

- Map B2
- Fort Christian: Map P3; 340-776-4566; Open 9am–4pm Mon–Fri
- Legislature Building: Map P3; 340-774-0880; Open 8am–5pm Mon–Fri
- Frederick Lutheran Church: Map P2; 340-776-1315; Open 7:30am–4:30pm Mon–Fri
- Government House: Map Q2; 340-774-0001; Open 8am–5pm Mon–Fri
- St. Thomas Synagogue: Map N2; 340-774-4312; Open 9am–4pm Mon–Fri; Visitors welcome to services 6:30 pm Fri & 10am Sat
- Seven Arches Museum: Map Q2; 340-774-9295; Open 10am–4pm daily; Adm $5
- Haagensen House: Map P2; Foot entrance off 99 Steps; 340-774-9605; Open 9am–noon daily; Adm $8

Top 10 Sights

1. Fort Christian
2. Legislature Building
3. Emancipation Garden
4. Frederick Lutheran Church
5. Old Warehouses
6. Government House
7. St. Thomas Synagogue
8. Seven Arches Museum
9. 99 Steps
10. Haagensen House

1 Fort Christian
Standing proud near the waterfront, the huge rust-colored Fort Christian *(right)* is the oldest building in St. Thomas. Built by the Danes to protect the island, its construction began in 1672. A small museum within has artifacts from the island's past.

2 Legislature Building
Originally a Danish police barracks, this building later housed the high school. It is now home to the territory's 15-member political body. You can attend sessions if you're wearing appropriate attire.

3 Emancipation Garden
This park commemorates the 1848 emancipation of the slaves. A bust of King Christian V *(above)* and a replica of Philadelphia's Liberty Bell sit among shaded benches, which provide a respite for tired sightseers. 🔊 *Map P3*

4 Frederick Lutheran Church
Built in 1820 as the Danish state church, the building *(left)* retains much of its original Neo-Classical and Gothic Revival character. Its gracious front steps allow folks to peek inside at its lovely stained-glass windows and bell tower. Visitors are welcome to the 9am Sunday services.

Old Warehouses

5 Main Street's stores originally served as warehouses in the sugar and rum trade. There was no waterfront highway, and ships used to back right up to the warehouses to take on cargo. ◈ *Map N2*

Government House

6 Built in 1867 for the Danish Colonial Council, this pretty building *(left)* now serves as the governor's office. The lower level, which displays four works by Impressionist painter and native son, Camille Pissarro, is open to visitors.

St. Thomas Synagogue

7 With a congregation that dates back to 1796, this synagogue *(above)* is the second oldest in the Caribbean. The gracious building dates to 1833 (two earlier buildings fell victim to fire). Its sand floor signifies the flight of Jews from Egypt.

Seven Arches Museum

8 The owner of this private home *(above)* welcomes visitors for a glimpse of early Danish life. A typical 18th-century Danish West Indian house, it features an expansive "welcoming arms" staircase supported by seven arches, and period pieces.

99 Steps

9 Built in the 18th century to connect the upper and lower parts of town, this staircase *(right)* actually has 103 steps of yellow ship-ballast brick. Continue up Government Hill for grand views from the old tower of Blackbeard's Castle, now part of a hotel *(see p113)*. ◈ *Map P2*

Haagensen House

10 This restored 19th-century home belonged to Danish banker and merchant Hans Haagensen. The bedrooms, sitting room, and veranda are furnished in period pieces. Typical of its time, it has a cookhouse and other outbuildings. You can also explore the adjacent herb garden.

Coral World, St. Thomas

Much more than an aquarium, Coral World gets you up close and personal with sea life without getting wet, although some of its activities afford adventurous opportunities for those willing to go into the water. While you can see it all in a couple of hours, it's a great place for both adults and kids to spend the whole day. In addition to its huge undersea observatory, tank exhibits, and shark-feeding experience, Coral World serves as a center for rehabilitating turtles and breeding seahorses, and has an extensive mangrove replanting project to help improve the eco-system in its neighborhood.

Parasailing

🌀 **For an unusual experience, drop your postcards in the Underwater Observatory mailbox –** they'll be stamped "Mailed Underwater at Coral World."

🍴 **You can lunch at Coral World's Shark Bar & Grill or Beach Café.**

• Map C2; Coki Point off Rte 38; 340-775-1555, 888-695-2073; www.coralworldvi.com; Open 9am–5pm daily; Adm $18 adults, $9 children, $52 family (for two adults & up to four children)
• Sea Trekkin': Must be over age 8 & weigh more than 80 pounds (36 kg); $50 in addition to Coral World adm
• Snuba: Minimum age 8; $60 for adults & $57 for children under 12 (incl Coral World adm)
• Parasailing: Caribbean Watersports at 340-775-9360 or www.viwatersports.com/parasail.htm; $60 for trips

Top 10 Sights

1. Undersea Observatory
2. Shark Shallows
3. Stingray Pool
4. Marine Gardens
5. Caribbean Reef Encounter
6. Tropical Nature Trail
7. Sea Trekkin'
8. Snuba
9. Parasailing
10. Scuba, Snorkel, or Swim at Coki Beach

1 Undersea Observatory

Coral World's centerpiece takes you 100 ft (30 m) out into the ocean and 15 ft (4 m) deep *(right)*. Look into the ocean through 24 huge windows and enjoy the ever-changing scene as colorful fish swim by.

2 Shark Shallows

A wide variety of Caribbean sharks, which may include lemon, reef, nurse, and Atlantic black-tip, swim in a large tank, viewable from the top and one side *(above)*. Children get a chance to pet a baby shark when staff members do their daily feeding.

3 Stingray Pool

It takes a careful eye to see a stingray buried in the sand, but those with patience are rewarded. Stingrays occasionally glide around the pool, looking like giant dinner plates gone adrift. Visitors are invited to feed the stingrays with the help of an aquarist.

Coral World's website often offers discount coupons

4 Marine Gardens

Twenty-one aquariums are home to an abundance of marine species *(above)*. Take your time to spot such creatures as the camouflaged scorpionfish, and look for crabs, tubeworms, and sea anemones on the reef.

Plan of Coral World

5 Caribbean Reef Encounter

In this 80,000-gallon (303,200-liter) tank that replicates the reefs just offshore Coral World, visitors can explore a huge variety of marine life. Interpretive panels explain how reefs form and the role they play in keeping fish alive.

6 Tropical Nature Trail

Land meets water on this trail. Aquatic plants sway in fresh-water pools, and tropical foliage fringes the walking paths. Keep your eyes peeled for bright green baby iguanas, hummingbirds, and yellow bananaquits.

7 Sea Trekkin'

Don a helmet hooked up to an air hose for this easy adventure on the ocean floor *(below)*. Your face and hair stay dry as you stroll around a reef in your bathing suit. There is a handrail to keep you on track.

8 Snuba

A Snuba adventure is a good way to go underwater without the fuss of scuba-diving. Swim over the ocean floor with ease on this half-hour tour, wearing mask, fins, and an airhose attached to a central supply.

9 Parasailing

Get a bird's-eye view of the ocean below as you soar 600 ft (180 m) up in the air while tethered to a boat. You won't get wet, but if you want to dip your toes in the sea, the captain is usually willing to oblige.

10 Scuba, Snorkel, or Swim at Coki Beach

Sitting adjacent to Coral World, lovely Coki Beach *(above)* is the ideal place to spend time sunning after your Coral World visit. If you want to be more active, rent dive and snorkel gear from Coral World's dive shop.

A guide accompanies groups on both the Sea Trekkin' and Snuba trips

⑩ BVI National Parks & Scenic Spots

Except for downtown Road Town, unspoiled is an apt word to describe the British Virgin Islands. There are scenic spots galore, but some merit special mention because the BVI government has taken serious steps to make sure they stay in their pristine state despite an increasing number of visitors. These small, special parks are for travelers who like to get off the beaten path. Poke about the land parks or take a dive trip to the parks' showcase, the Wreck of the Rhone.

Yellow alder flower

Spring Bay National Park, Virgin Gorda

🌀 **Sign on with a dive operator for a trip to the Wreck of the Rhone NP, if you don't have your own or charter boat.**

• *BVI National Parks Trust: Map H4; 61 Main St, Road Town; 340-494-2069; www.bvinationalparkstrust.org* • *Sage Mountain NP: Map G5; Park entrance off Ridge Rd; Open dawn–dusk daily* • *J.R. O'Neal Botanic Gardens: Map H4; Botanic Station Rd, Road Town; Open 8:30am–4:30pm Mon–Sat* • *Callwood Rum Distillery: Map G4; North Coast Rd, Cane Garden Bay; Hrs vary*

Top 10 Sights

1. Sage Mountain National Park, Tortola
2. J.R. O'Neal Botanic Gardens, Tortola
3. Mount Healthy National Park, Tortola
4. Callwood Rum Distillery, Tortola
5. Long Bay, Beef Island
6. Coppermine National Park, Virgin Gorda
7. Spring Bay National Park, Virgin Gorda
8. Gorda Peak National Park, Virgin Gorda
9. The Baths National Park, Virgin Gorda
10. The Wreck of the Rhone National Park, off Salt Island

1 Sage Mountain National Park, Tortola
At 1,716 ft (515 m), Sage Mountain is the tallest in the Virgin Islands. Most of the park *(below)* sits above 1,000 ft (300 m), which allows rainforest species to grow. Hike the paths that crisscross its 92 acres.

2 J.R. O'Neal Botanic Gardens, Tortola
This small garden provides a shady respite from the rigors of touring Road Town. Formerly the island's agri-cultural experiment station, the park is home to over 62 species of palms as well as many other varieties of tropical plants. The grounds include a cactus garden.

3 Mount Healthy National Park, Tortola
Dating to 1798, this estate has an old stone windmill as its heart, the only one left in the BVI. Nearby are ruins of the overseers' quarters and boiling house, overlooking Tortola's north shore. ◎ *Map H4*

4 Callwood Rum Distillery, Tortola

Privately owned, this tiny distillery *(above)* dates to the 18th century. It is the only place in the BVI that still produces rum. Stop by for a tour and bring home a few bottles.

5 Long Bay, Beef Island

This lovely beach offers acres of solitude, particularly at its western end. Shell aficionados can while away a few hours scouring the beach. You'll see Little and Great Camanoe as well as Marina Cay and Scrub Island across the water. ◈ *Map J4*

6 Coppermine National Park, Virgin Gorda

Cornish miners worked the mines here in the mid-1800s, but there's evidence of earlier use by the Spanish. The ruins of a copper mine chimney stand by the shore *(below)* with a boiling house, cistern, and mine shaft nearby. ◈ *Map L4*

7 Spring Bay National Park, Virgin Gorda

A gorgeous strand of sand and calm coves make this the perfect place to stop for a swim. Snorkeling is excellent as well. The beach has a swing set and picnic tables. ◈ *Map L4*

9 The Baths National Park, Virgin Gorda

Boulders *(below)* as large as 40 ft (12 m) form caves that can be explored on foot and with snorkel. This is a busy area, a 10-minute hike down from the road. ◈ *Map L4*

8 Gorda Peak National Park, Virgin Gorda

The wooden tower on the 1,370-ft (410-m) Gorda Peak extends the views as far south as St. Croix, some 50 miles (80 km) away. The park has several species of flora and fauna, including the Virgin Islands gecko. ◈ *Map L3*

10 The Wreck of the Rhone National Park, off Salt Island

The mail ship *Rhone* went down in 1867 when a hurricane dashed it against the rocks off Salt Island. Any treasures have long since been looted, but swim through its hulk for a great show of marine life *(above)*. ◈ *Map J5*

🔟 Sailing in the British Virgin Islands

One of the world's premier sailing destinations, the BVI offers mariners the opportunity to drop anchor at pristine, deserted harbors as well as popular ones with a thriving bar and restaurant scene. The waters are warm, the seas usually on the calm side, the trade winds normally brisk, and the scenery gorgeous. Sail bare boats, which put you at the helm, or crewed ones, which come with a licensed captain and chef to conjure up gourmet meals in the boat's galley.

2 Jost Van Dyke
Foxy's bar at this tiny island *(above)* is legendary, but there are many other similar spots at Great and Little Harbours and White Bay. You can clear BVI Customs at Great Harbour *(see p91).* 🔊 *Map G3*

The Baths, Virgin Gorda

🛥 Major companies such as The Moorings and Sunsail, as well as smaller ones in Tortola, rent both bare and crewed sailboats. Look on the Internet for a suitable charter broker. Your local travel agent can also book these trips.

Charter brokers will match you with a like-minded captain and crew.

If you're chartering a bare boat, the charter company will provision your boat for a fee.

• The Moorings: 888-952-8420; www.moorings.com
• Sunsail: 800-327-2276 in the US, 023-9222-2333 in the UK; www.sunsail.com/usa, www.sunsail.com/uk
• Lynn Jachney Charters: 800-223-2050; www. lynnjachneycharters.com

Top 10 Anchorages

1. The Dogs
2. Jost Van Dyke
3. Marina Cay
4. Sandy Cay
5. Norman Island
6. Cane Garden Bay, Tortola
7. Salt Island
8. Cooper Island
9. The Baths, Virgin Gorda
10. North Sound, Virgin Gorda

1 The Dogs
While sailing between North Sound, Virgin Gorda, and Jost Van Dyke, stop by the small island group known as the Dogs for a peaceful anchorage with good diving. The best anchorages are in the bays west of Kitchen Point on George Dog and on the south side of Great Dog. 🔊 *Map K3*

Sailing, North Sound

3 Marina Cay
Nestled in a sheltered, emerald-green lagoon and ringed by soft, white sand, Marina Cay *(left)* is home to Pusser's Restaurant *(see p116),* which attracts sailors as well as landlubbers who catch the ferry from Trellis Bay for salty cama-raderie and good food. The island is fringed by coral; boats enter through the north side channel *(see p90).* 🔊 *Map J4*

Crewed charters that sail the BVI leave from St. Thomas in nearby USVI or Tortola, but most bare boats depart from Tortola

4 Sandy Cay
Make a day stop at this deserted island for great snorkeling and strolling on the white beach. Deep water almost to the shore allows boats to come in close. Summer anchoring is best since winter swells can make it a rolly stay (see p91). ✎ Map H3

5 Norman Island
Rumored to be a site of buried treasures, this island (above) features a popular anchorage known as the Bight, home to the floating William Thornton restaurant and the shoreside Pirates Bight. Enjoy good snorkeling here (see p90). ✎ Map H6

6 Cane Garden Bay, Tortola
One of the islands' hottest anchorages, Cane Garden Bay (below) has several popular bars and restaurants as well as the historic Callwood Rum Distillery (see p21). A great stop for stretching your sea legs along the long, sandy beach (see p82). ✎ Map G4

7 Salt Island
Use the moorings near the offshore wreck of the Rhone to explore the undersea wreck with mask and fins. Or go ashore at Salt Island's Lee Bay or Salt Pond Bay to visit ancient salt ponds still in use for harvesting salt (see p90). ✎ Map J5

8 Cooper Island
Drop anchor at Cooper Island's Manchioneel Bay, for lunch or dinner at the very casual Cooper Island Beach Club (see p113). The small resort has a dinghy dock to make access easy for sailors and a glorious beach ideal for sunbathing. ✎ Map K5

9 The Baths, Virgin Gorda
While the Baths (right) can get quite crowded with dinghies going back and forth to boats, it's worth a stop to snorkel among the huge boulders that form small grottos. Swells from the north may make overnight anchorages somewhat unpleasant during the winter months (see p89). ✎ Map L4

10 North Sound, Virgin Gorda
North Sound is home to a handful of resorts, all with bars and most catering to sailors. Distances between resorts are small, so it's easy to bar-hop in your dinghy. But designate a nondrinker to take the helm (see p89 & p91). ✎ Map M3

Dive & Snorkel Trips

The Virgin Islands are a diver's dream come true. While snorkeling gives you a bird's-eye view of the vividly colored reefs below, diving lets you get close to the marine life on the reefs. Wave your finger near a sea anemone and watch it close, look a tarpon in the eye, or glide through a school of fry. Near-shore reefs allow for beach dives while many companies run boat trips for an off-shore experience. Some offer diving and snorkeling on the same trip, making a perfect combo for groups with divers and non-divers who want to snorkel.

Kids learning to scuba-dive

Dive operators offer both one- and two-tank dives. Companies also rent all gear. While you'll need certification from PADI or NAUI to go on most dives, novices can take dive courses, called resort courses. Divers can take advanced courses that include rescue diving.

- St. Croix: Anchor Dive Center, Salt River; 340-778-1522; www. anchordivestcroix.com
- St. Thomas: Aqua Action, Secret Harbour Beach Resort, Nazareth; 340-775-6285; www. aadivers.com
- St. John: Low Key Watersports, Wharfside Village, Cruz Bay; 340-693-8999; www. divelowkey.com
- Tortola: Underwater Safaris, Moorings-Mariner Inn, Wickhams Cay II, Road Town; 284-494-3235; www. underwatersafaris.com
- Virgin Gorda: Dive BVI, VG Yacht Harbor, Spanish Town & Leverick Bay, North Sound; 284-495-5513; www.divebvi.com

Top 10 Dive Sites

1. Buck Island Reef National Monument, St. Croix
2. Frederiksted Pier, St. Croix
3. The Wall, St. Croix
4. Carval Rock, off St. John
5. Grass & Mingo Cays, off St. John
6. Cow & Calf, off St. Thomas
7. Wreck of the WIT Shoal II, off St. Thomas
8. Wreck of the General Rogers, off St. Thomas
9. Wreck of the Rhone, off Salt Island
10. The Indians, BVI

1 Buck Island Reef National Monument, St. Croix

Located about 5 miles (8 km) offshore from Christiansted, this marine garden is reached only by charter sail or power boat. While you can dive its colorful reefs, this site provides a perfect learn-to-snorkel experience. Charter boats also stop at Buck Island's sandy beach on the west end. ✪ *Map E4*

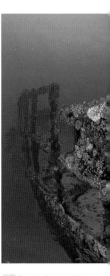

2 Frederiksted Pier, St. Croix

Marine life abounds, but seahorses are the main reason to dive this site. For safety's sake, take a trip with one of Frederiksted's dive operators. The dive master will help you find the seahorses. ✪ *Map A5*

3 The Wall, St. Croix

The coral- and sponge-covered Wall *(left)* runs along the island's north shore. It drops off from about 30 ft (9 m) to thousands, luring divers with varying degrees of ability. In some places, it runs so close to the shore that you can do a beach dive. ✪ *Map B4*

PADI stands for Professional Association of Dive Instructors and NAUI for National Association of Underwater Instructors

4 Carval Rock, off St. John

Located about 4 miles (6 km) north of St. John, Carval Rock *(left)* juts up into the ocean looking like an old-time ship called a carval. Fish swim among dramatic rock formations and bright coral reefs at depths of 20 to 80 ft (6–24 m). ⚓ *Map D1*

5 Grass & Mingo Cays, off St. John

Part of a small chain of cays north of St. John, these tiny islands are surrounded by a kaleidoscopic marine life. Turtles visit often *(below)*. Little or no current keeps visibility high. ⚓ *Map D2*

6 Cow & Calf, off St. Thomas

Barely breaking the water off the southeast end of St. Thomas, these two rocks feature tunnels, archways, and overhangs, all at depths less than 40 ft (12 m). Multihued fish or the occasional nurse shark swim along with you as you navigate this dive site. ⚓ *Map C3*

7 Wreck of the WIT Shoal II, off St. Thomas

Explore the interior of this 327-ft (98-m) World War II landing ship *(above)*, sitting off St. Thomas's south side. The coral-encrusted wreck is home to shiny fish. ⚓ *Map A3*

8 Wreck of the General Rogers, off St. Thomas

Located off St. Thomas's north coast, this 120-ft (36-m) wreck of a US Coast Guard boat houses a rich marine life, including tube sponges, hard and soft corals, and bristleworms. Look out for barracuda. ⚓ *Map C2*

9 Wreck of the Rhone, off Salt Island

Sitting in two parts at 15 to 75 ft (4–22 m) deep after it sank in 1867, this wreck *(above)* attracts undersea explorers from both the USVI and BVI. A good diving and snorkeling site *(see p21 & p90)*. ⚓ *Map J5*

10 The Indians, BVI

Near Peter and Norman Islands, four jagged pinnacles, with a base sitting 50 ft (15 m) down, break the surface. Swim through canyons and grottos that contain brilliant corals, house varieties of fish, and are visited by hawksbill turtles. ⚓ *Map H6*

Virgin Islands Top 10

Beach Resorts

Placing glorious beaches right at your doorstep, the resorts strung out along the islands' shorelines run the gamut from exclusive luxury hotels to campgrounds where you can rough it out. Package deals abound in these places, many of which are family-oriented. Most have so many amenities that you need not leave the resort at all. Spend lazy hours sunning on soft white sands or enjoy the range of watersport activities as well as the fine or casual dining your hotel offers.

Bolongo Bay Beach Club, St. Thomas

Sunbathing at the Buccaneer Hotel beach

🐚 Beach resorts run from posh to casual, so pack accordingly. Some require a jacket for men after 6pm; at others you can get by with shorts and t-shirts no matter what the time of day.

When picking a resort, it really pays to do your homework. If you want lots of activities included in your room rate, look for that specific information. Most resorts include things such as snorkel gear, sailboat, and kayak use, but some charge a small fee.

• Villas of Fort Recovery Estate: Map G5; Box 239, Tortola, BVI; 800-367-8455, 284-495-4354; www.fortrecovery.com; $$$$$ (incl breakfast)
• Details, including map references, for the rest of the resorts listed here are on the pages given in text

Top 10 Resorts

1. The Buccaneer Hotel, St. Croix
2. Caneel Bay Resort, St. John
3. Cinnamon Bay Campground, St. John
4. Bolongo Bay Beach Club, St. Thomas
5. Grand Bay Palace Spa & Resort, St. Thomas
6. Villas of Fort Recovery Estate, Tortola
7. Little Dix Bay, Virgin Gorda
8. Biras Creek Hotel, Virgin Gorda
9. Nail Bay Resort, Virgin Gorda
10. Peter Island Resort & Yacht Club

2 Caneel Bay Resort, St. John

With seven great beaches – one for each day of the week, as the resort says – a stay at Caneel *(left)* provides superb vacationing. Most rooms are on the beach, with a few in the gardens. There are three fine restaurants *(see p112)*.

1 The Buccaneer Hotel, St. Croix

Located on St. Croix's north shore, this hotel has it all – fine beaches, plentiful watersports, golf, tennis, as well as excellent dining. The hillside rooms have better views, but the beachfront ones put you closer to the sand. With Christiansted close by, shopping excursions are easy as well *(see p112)*.

3 Cinnamon Bay Campground, St. John

This beachfront campground in the Virgin Islands National Park has tents, cottages, and bare sites for campers who bring their own tents. Facilities are close to the accommodations. Apart from swimming, snorkeling, and other watersports, it offers hiking and a casual restaurant *(see p115)*.

4 Bolongo Bay Beach Club, St. Thomas

The all-inclusive and semi-inclusive options at this casual beachfront resort *(left)* provide good value for families. All-inclusive plans include all meals and drinks. With semi-inclusive, you get an extensive continental breakfast. Both plans include a wide array of watersports. Rooms at this appealing resort range from motel-style to condominiums *(see p115)*.

5 Grand Bay Palace Spa & Resort, St. Thomas

Rooms sit beachfront and hillside at this mega resort *(above)* on St. Thomas's south shore. It offers plenty of watersports and everything else but golf, and that's only a 10-minute drive away. Off-season packages can make this hotel a good deal *(see p112)*.

6 Villas of Fort Recovery Estate, Tortola

Tucked between the road and the beach on Tortola's south shore, this small resort has an old stone fort as its centerpiece and lush foliage surrounding its suites and villas. En suite kitchens make this a good choice for independent travelers.

7 Little Dix Bay, Virgin Gorda

A staff that attends to every detail ensures that a stay at Little Dix Bay provides the ultimate in tropical vacations. You'll find tennis, watersports, a fitness center, and nightly movies, but many guests spend their days in a chaise *(see p112)*.

8 Biras Creek Hotel, Virgin Gorda

Enjoy garden walks, snorkeling, a Sunfish sail, and the lovely strand of white sand that fronts this restful hotel *(above)*, reachable only by boat (there's a launch service). While away the day with a good book, rising to dine on gourmet fare at the restaurant *(see p112)*.

9 Nail Bay Resort, Virgin Gorda

Three beaches, excellent snorkeling, tennis, and lovely views are on offer at this small resort. Rooms and villas climb the hills above the beach. Even the least expensive rooms have mini-kitchens, a plus for visitors who like to eat in some of the time *(see p117)*.

10 Peter Island Resort & Yacht Club

With five beaches on its own island, this resort *(left)* attracts guests who like privacy. Enjoy watersports or a massage during the day and fine dining every night in its sophisticated tropical ambience *(see p112)*.

Following pages **Wrasses and horse-eye jacks flitting amid coral at Cow Rock, off St. Thomas**

Left **Bacchus, St. Croix** Center **Chateau Bordeaux, St. John** Right **Sugar Mill Restaurant, Tortola**

🔟 Big Splurge Restaurants

1 Kendrick's, St. Croix
Innovative cuisine is the hallmark of Kendrick's, a cozy bistro tucked into a downtown courtyard. The chef dresses up simple fare such as king crab cakes with a lemon pepper *aïoli* and veal *scallopini* with grilled portobello mushrooms and fontina cheese *(see p61)*.

2 Restaurant Bacchus, St. Croix
A sophisticated ambience, an excellent wine list, and an imaginative menu make for a tempting restaurant choice. Go for dishes such as baked chicken with lemon and rosemary or a pork prime rib with barbecue sauce *(see p61)*.

3 Asolare, St. John
The contemporary Asian-inspired cuisine focuses on seafood dishes such as baked catfish in coconut and plum curry sauce. The food alone makes it a must-do, but go also for the feel of this old stone house overlooking Cruz Bay and the spectacular sunset views *(see p69)*.

4 Chateau Bordeaux, St. John
White lace tablecloths, a rustic interior, and fine views set the stage for a lovely dining experience. Basics such as fish, lamb, and beef are accompanied by flavorsome sauces. The chocolate cups filled with berries and Chambord are heavenly *(see p69)*.

5 Hervé Restaurant, St. Thomas
Hervé conjures up fine French food with a Caribbean flair at this hillside restaurant in downtown Charlotte Amalie. There's veal roulade and spinach-stuffed lamb chops, but try red snapper with Creole sauce or the Caribbean lobster flamed with Armagnac for a bit of local flavor *(see p79)*.

6 Virgilio's Restaurant, St. Thomas
Located in an old stone warehouse in Charlotte Amalie's shopping district, this is where the island's movers and shakers dine. Eavesdropping is a fine art here. Pasta comes in many

View of Cruz Bay from Asolare, St. John

For more restaurants See pp32–3, 36–7, 61, 69, 79, 85 & 93 forms – the seafood and linguine is a sure bet. Or try the chicken served in lemon sauce *(see p79)*.

7 Romano's Restaurant, St. Thomas

The neighborhood isn't much, but step inside Romano's for North Italian cuisine at its best. With white tablecloths and owner Tony Romano's artwork on the walls, the atmosphere is equally fabulous. The chicken breast with mushrooms, mozzarella, garlic, white wine, and tomato is divine *(see p79)*.

8 Sugar Mill Restaurant, Tortola

Food writers Jeff and Jinx Morgan have created one of the island's most enchanting restaurants in an old sugar mill. The food matches the alfresco air, with Caribbean-inspired dishes predominating. The menu changes daily, but pumpkin soup and spicy chicken with pineapple salsa often appear *(see p85)*.

9 Brandywine Bay, Tortola

Candlelit tables and an extensive view serve as the backdrop for Tuscan-style food. The chef uses plenty of fresh herbs and foods to create exquisite dishes. Try the local swordfish if you're in the mood for fish or the duck with a fresh berry sauce *(see p85)*.

10 Little Dix Bay Pavilion, Virgin Gorda

A sophisticated menu that highlights fish, chicken, and veal accompanied by inspired side dishes and sauces attracts more than just hotel guests. Stunning ambience and attentive service. ⊗ *Map L4 • Little Dix Bay, outside Spanish Town • 284-495-5555* • *www.littledixbay.com • $$$$$*

Top 10 Restaurants by the Sea

1 Blue Moon, St. Croix
This funky little place on the waterfront has jazz on Sunday afternoons *(see p61)*.

2 Off the Wall, St. Croix
Enjoy burgers and beer at this casual spot *(see p61)*.

3 Panini Beach, St. John
The fine Italian fare here includes its namesake pressed *panini* sandwiches *(see p69)*.

4 Skinny Legs Bar & Restaurant, St. John
A yachtie hangout with a sail for part of its roof. The menu runs to fish burgers *(see p69)*.

5 Miss Lucy's, St. John
Dine on Caribbean cuisine at the water's edge under seagrape trees *(see p69)*.

6 Agave Terrace, St. Thomas
Seafood done a dozen ways and a lovely ambience are the highlights here *(see p79)*.

7 Blue Moon Café, St. Thomas
Sitting almost in the sand, this charming place offers tropical twists on its menu *(see p79)*.

8 Eclipse, Tortola
A grazing menu allows you to sample a little of everything at this seafront place *(see p85)*.

9 Giorgio's Table, Virgin Gorda
Features Mediterranean and Italian fare as well as fresh Caribbean lobster and fish. ⊗ *Map L3 • Mahoe Bay • 284-495-5684 • $$$$$*

10 Sandcastle, Jost Van Dyke
Superb beachfront location, with your choice of fish, fowl, or beef done Caribbean style. ⊗ *Map G3 • White Bay • 284-495-9888 • Closed Fri • $$$*

Left **Glenda's, St. Thomas** Center **Hercules' Paté Delight, St. John** Right **Roti Palace, Tortola**

TOP 10 West Indian Restaurants

1 Harvey's Restaurant, St. Croix

Sarah Harvey dishes up great West Indian food at her unassuming restaurant. Yummy whelks in butter sauce, fish and *fungi* (a cornmeal and okra dish), and goat stew served with a variety of side dishes are the highlights. The helpings are huge. ◈ *Map D5 • 11B Company St, Christiansted • 340-773-3433 • Closed Sun, no dinner • $*

Harvey's Restaurant, St. Croix

2 Comfee's West Indian Kitchen, St. John

Stop at this kiosk for the superb patés. Turnovers are filled with well-seasoned lobster, saltfish, or ground beef, called meat in the islands, and fried till extra crispy. ◈ *Map D2 • Next to Julius E. Sprauve School at intersection of Centerline Rd (Rte 10) & Rte 104, Cruz Bay • 340-714-5262 • Closed Sun, no dinner • $*

3 Hercules' Paté Delight, St. John

Hercules cooks up fish, chicken, and more, all well seasoned with fresh peppers, onions, and tomatoes at this hole-in-the-wall spot. His hold-in-the-hand patés make delicious on-the-go lunches. While you can eat at one of the few roadside tables, traffic noise and odors make take-out a better option. ◈ *Map D2 • Boulon Center Rd, Cruz Bay • 340-776-6352 • Closed Sun, no dinner • $*

4 Glenda's Caribbean Spot, St. Thomas

With a menu that runs to Caribbean lobster and fresh local fish broiled, boiled, or fried, Glenda's Caribbean Spot dishes up scrumptious West Indian fare in an extremely casual setting. All dishes come with large helpings of plantains, rice and peas (locally called rice and beans), and *fungi*. ◈ *Map C2 • Smith Bay Rd (Rte 38), Smith Bay • 340-775-2699 • $$$*

5 Lillian's Caribbean Grill, St. Thomas

Stop by Lillian's Caribbean Grill for local dishes such as rice and beans as well as a cool drink of passion fruit juice, sea moss, or ginger beer. For less adventurous eaters, Lillian's also serves hamburgers and barbecued ribs along with fries. Customers can sit inside or out under shady umbrella tables. ◈ *Map P2 • Grand Galleria Courtyard, Charlotte Amalie • 340-774-7900 • http://pws.prserv.net/lillian • Closed Sun • $*

Comfee's, St. John

For price ranges **See p61**

6 C&F Restaurant, Tortola

Lobster, conch in lime butter sauce, and curry are the highlights, as is the fine barbecue. The decor is on the modest side, but the food is always tasty. ⊗ Map H4 • Purcell Estate, Road Town • 284-494-4941 • $$$

7 Roti Palace, Tortola

Coming north with Trinidadian immigrants, roti is a flat bread filled with delicious things. This unassuming place sitting up a hill does curried chicken with potatoes well, and other varieties such as lobster and vegetables. ⊗ Map H4 • Off Main St on Russell Hill, ask directions, Road Town • 284-494-4196 • $

8 Mrs. Scatliffe's Restaurant, Tortola

The delicious West Indian fare served on the upstairs front porch of Mrs. Scatliffe's home includes superb pumpkin soup and chicken with coconut rice. Reservations by 5pm mandatory. ⊗ Map H4 • Carrot Bay • 284-495-4556 • No credit cards • $$$

9 Fisher's Cove, Virgin Gorda

This alfresco restaurant gives a Caribbean twist to standards such as duck, steak, and lobster. Make a meal out of the divine pumpkin soup and the crisp conch fritters. ⊗ Map L4 • Lee Rd, Spanish Town • 284-495-5252 • $$$$

10 Abe's by the Sea, Jost Van Dyke

A very casual spot, Abe's is famous for its Wednesday night pig roast, held only during the winter season. At other times, you'll have to settle for fresh lobster, conch, fish, chicken, or the tasty barbecue. ⊗ Map H3 • Little Harbour • 284-495-9329 • $$$$

Top 10 Kid-Friendly Restaurants

1 McDonald's
⊗ Wheatley Center & Frenchtown, St. Thomas; Orange Grove, Villa La Reine & Sunshine Mall, St. Croix • $

2 Pizza Hut
⊗ Veterans Dr & Wheatley Center, St. Thomas; Christiansted & Villa La Reine, St. Croix • $

3 Cheeseburgers in Paradise, St. Croix
Casual outdoor dining. ⊗ Map E4 • East End Rd (Rte 82) • 340-773-1119 • $$

4 Breezes, St. Croix
Kids go for the burgers and fries. ⊗ Map D4 • Rte 752, Club St. Croix, Golden Rock • 340-773-7077 • $$$

5 Uncle Joe's Barbecue, St. John
Spicy barbecued chicken and ribs at this tiny spot. ⊗ Map D2 • North Shore Rd (Rte 20), Cruz Bay • 340-693-8806 • $

6 Shipwreck Landing, St. John
Fish, chicken, or pasta dinner. ⊗ Map E2 • Rte 107, outside Coral Bay • 340-693-5640 • $$$

7 Delly Deck, St. Thomas
Perfect for a quick lunch for families. ⊗ Map B2 • Havensight Mall, Havensight Rd (Rte 30) • 340-776-9943 • $

8 Skyworld, Tortola
Lunch best for kids, more elegant later (see p85).

9 The Pub, Tortola
Pub-style food. ⊗ Map H4 • Waterfront Dr, Road Town • 284-494-2608 • $$

10 The Bath & the Turtle, Virgin Gorda
Pizzas, pasta, and burgers. ⊗ Map L4 • Virgin Gorda Yacht Harbor, Spanish Town • 284-495-5239 • $$$

For more restaurants **See pp30–31, 36–7, 61, 69, 79, 85 & 93**

Left **Conch fritters** Right **Lobster**

Top 10 Local Food & Drink

1 Conch Fritters
Crunchy on the outside and creamy on the inside, these spicy conch and batter morsels are deep fried. While they're traditionally served as first courses or snacks, light eaters can make a meal of them. Every cook prepares them differently, but the more conch the better.

2 Goatwater

You'll find this tasty goat stew on the menu at only the most local of West Indian restaurants in the islands. Cooked with the same type of goat you see wandering along the roadsides, its other ingredients include onions, garlic, tomatoes, and the cook's own special spices.

Chef at Hercules' Paté enjoying one of his own

3 Hot Sauce
Conjured up in local kitchens, hot sauce adds extra bite to any dish. It's made of fresh hot peppers, onions, and whatever else strikes the cook's fancy. Every one is different; try several of them. A bottle keeps forever in your refrigerator even though the color may change.

4 Kallaloo or Callaloo
The islands' famous spicy soup *kallaloo* has as many spellings as ingredients. With greens, usually spinach or whatever's available, as its base, the soup also includes a generous dose of okra, maybe ham or fish, and, of course, whatever seasonings the cook likes to use.

5 Lobster
Caribbean lobsters lack the claws of their northern cousins, but they're still a sweet, succulent seafood, served in several ways in the Virgin Islands. The simplest lobster dish, just drizzled with melted butter and served in the shell, may be the best, but many people prefer it stuffed with crabmeat.

Hot sauce

Locating Local Food
Look for local cuisine at tiny, tucked-away West Indian restaurants. Events such as Carnival celebrations on all the islands are a good bet. At those festivals, you'll find dishes seldom featured on the menu no matter how local the restaurant. To find the best food, look for the longest line out front.

For West Indian restaurants **See pp32–3**

Maubi
6 A spicy drink, *maubi* is fermented from *maubi* bark with generous helpings of sugar, dried orange peel, cinnamon, and cloves added. It's an acquired taste, and folks either love it or hate it. *Maubi* is found on the menu only at local restaurants.

Patés
7 Not the creamy meat dish made of goose or duck found in fine restaurants, Caribbean patés are turnovers stuffed with a spicy lobster, conch, chicken, or beef filling, then deep fried. Not for the cholesterol-shy, these delicious treats make great quick lunches or snacks.

Ole Wife
8 Usually served boiled with onions and spices, ole wife is officially called triggerfish or moonfish. Most cooks just take a little of this and some of that to conjure up their version of this tasty catch of the day.

Johnnycake
9 Found on just about all West Indian menus, this staple is simply a deep-fried, flattened biscuit (dumpling). Johnnycakes are usually served hot, but residents take them cold in their lunches. If you happen on an event with food demonstrations, you may see cooks rolling them out in the kitchen.

Johnnycake

Tarts
10 Tarts are the Virgin Islands' word for one-crust pies, often filled with coconut, guava, or other fruits. A word of caution: Caribbean cooks have a heavy hand with the sugar, so tarts are often sweeter than you expect.

Top 10 Rums

Appleton
1 The Jamaican company Appleton has several rums, including the premium 21-year-old Appleton Estate rum.

Don Q
2 One of Puerto Rico's gifts to the rum industry, Don Q manufactures many varieties – its Light is quite popular.

Cruzan
3 Light and Dark are staple Cruzan rums but this St. Croix-based company *(see p57)* also makes higher quality rums.

Callwood's Arundel
4 Found only in Tortola, this 80 proof spirit, brewed at a beachfront distillery *(see p21)*, packs quite a punch.

Flavored Rums
5 With additives such as vanilla, coconut, pineapple, and many others, flavored rums make popular apéritifs.

Mount Gay
6 The Barbados-based Mount Gay has many varieties, but its Eclipse is most often found on island shelves.

Myer's
7 Of its numerous rum varieties, the Jamaican Myer's Dark is one of the most popular with rum connoisseurs.

Pusser's
8 Sold only at Pusser's stores in Tortola and Virgin Gorda, this rum gained its reputation in the British Navy.

Rhum Barbancourt
9 Made in Haiti, this premium rum comes in many varieties, which depend on the length of aging.

Ron del Barrilito
10 Limited in distribution, this Puerto Rican company makes rum eagerly sought by rum aficionados.

Left **Divi Carina Bay Casino, St. Croix** Right **Bomba Shack, Tortola**

TOP 10 Party Hearty Spots

1 Divi Carina Bay Casino, St. Croix

While you can spend hours at the gaming tables in the Divi, it is the only casino in the USVI, it is also one of the hottest nightspots around with live music almost every night. The casino stays open until at least 4am all week. ◈ *Map F4 • Divi Carina Bay Beach Resort, South Shore Rd (Rte 60), Turner Hole • 340-773-9700*

2 Moonraker Bar, St. Croix

Open Wednesday to Saturday, this Christiansted nightspot brings in a youthful crowd on Saturdays when DJs spin great dance music. Saturday is also ladies night, with a discount on drinks for women. On Wednesdays, the crowd enjoys karaoke. Moonraker is open until 2am all nights. ◈ *Map D5 • 43A Queen Cross St, Christiansted • 340-713-8025*

3 Duffy's Love Shack, St. John

The island's younger folks gather in droves at this popular nightspot, where the music is very loud, the drinks come with names such as Jaws, and the decor is straight out of the jungle. The late night Little Bites menu offers delicious munchies such as a lava bowl of guacamole. ◈ *Map D2 • Veste Gade, Cruz Bay • 340-776-6065 • www.duffysloveshack.com*

4 Woody's Seafood Saloon, St. John

The crowd that frequents this tiny bar and restaurant for late afternoon happy hours often overflows onto the sidewalk. It's a hot spot for sailors, drawn by cheap beers and the convivial ambience both inside and out. ◈ *Map D2 • On street with no name that leads up from the dock, Cruz Bay • 340-779-4625 • www.woodysseafood.com*

5 Fred's Bar & Restaurant, St. John

Fred's brings out black and white residents, and visitors of all ethnic origins, no matter what their age, to dance away the night to reggae and other sounds. The place doesn't look like much, but it can get hopping on Wednesday and Friday nights. ◈ *Map D2 • King St, across from Lemon Tree Mall, Cruz Bay • 340-776-6363*

6 Duffy's Love Shack, St. Thomas

Sitting in the parking lot of a shopping center, this hot spot shakes, rattles, and rolls till the wee hours. Drinks sport whimsical names such as Revenge of Godzilla. Like its sister spot in St. John, St. Thomas' Duffy's too has an interesting Little Bites menu. ◈ *Map C2 • Red Hook Shopping Center, Red Hook Rd (Rte 32), Red Hook • 340-779-2080 • www.duffysloveshack.com*

Cocktail at Duffy's, St. John

In all the islands, some restaurants may be closed for several weeks in August, September, and October

7 The Greenhouse, St. Thomas

The island's youthful crowd congregates here for live or DJ rock and other kinds of music. It's the place to mix and mingle as well as a big sailor hangout. The Greenhouse starts to heat up when the sun goes down, but by day it is a busy family restaurant. ◎ Map N3 • Veterans Dr (Rte 30), Charlotte Amalie • 340-774-7998

8 Hard Rock Café, St. Thomas

Like its fellow Hard Rock Cafés around the world, the St. Thomas one has blaring music and sports videos at all hours. Popular with cruise ship tourists who come during the day to sample the extensive lunch menu, the place also attracts locals and hotel guests who like its late night rocking ambience. ◎ Map N3 • Veterans Dr (Rte 30), Charlotte Amalie • 340-777-5555

9 Bomba Shack, Tortola

As its name suggests, this sizzling spot is just a collection of ramshackle boards on the beach. Bomba's legendary full moon parties are not to be missed if you like huge crowds and don't mind the sale of, shall we say, less-than-legal substances that happens nearby. ◎ Map G5 • North Coast Rd, Apple Bay • 284-495-4148

10 Foxy's, Jost Van Dyke

Yachties of all ages gather to hear the famous Foxy Callwood play calypso and more on his guitar, as well as music by local bands. A big party spot, this open-air bar is famous for hosting various regattas (see also p45). If you arrive early, enjoy a lobster dinner (see p93).

Top 10 Places to Listen to Music

1 The Buccaneer Hotel, St. Croix
Cocktail hour piano music segues into jazz, folk, and more (see p112).

2 Carambola Beach Resort, St. Croix
Jazz at the Sunday brunch, various bands on Wednesday and Fridays. ◎ Map B5 • Off North Shore Rd (Rte 80), Davis Bay • 340-778-3800

3 Caneel Bay Resort, St. John
This hotel's Beach Bar has a variety of music every night in winter (see p112).

4 Westin Resort, St. John
Jazz or piano plays almost every night at Chloe & Bernard's (see p69) in this upscale resort (see p115).

5 Epernay, St. Thomas
On Fridays and Saturdays, this posh restaurant becomes a late-night club (see p79).

6 Ritz-Carlton, St. Thomas
Relax at the Living Room with an après dinner cigar and live music (see p112).

7 Baywinds, St. Thomas
Live island-style music or karaoke in winter (see p112).

8 Smugglers, St. Thomas
Jazz or classical music most nights, with jazz at Sunday brunch (see p112).

9 Long Bay Beach Resort, Tortola
Listen to island-style music at the hotel's open-air Beach Café (see p117).

10 Little Dix Bay, Virgin Gorda
The lovely Pavilion restaurant offers diverse entertainment in winter (see p31).

Virgin Islands' Top 10

Left **Snorkeling near Buck Island, St. Croix** Right **Shark shallows, Coral World, St. Thomas**

🔟 Things for Kids

1 Fort Christianvaern, St. Croix

With lots of space to roam, the centerpiece of Christiansted National Historic Site gives kids a glimpse into history and a place to expend some energy. The park rangers are quick to answer children's questions *(see p8 & p57)*.

2 Day Sail to Buck Island Reef National Monument, St. Croix

A day sail is the perfect way to introduce children to sailing. Kids get to hoist sails and assist the captain at the wheel. Once at Buck Island, the crew will help them explore the reef with a snorkel, mask, and fins *(see p60).* ◈ *Your hotel will recommend their favorite charter captain*

3 Hike Cinnamon Bay Ruins Trail, St. John

This easy half-mile (1-km) loop trail across from Cinnamon Bay Campground on the North Shore Road takes you through sugar factory ruins and past an old cemetery that dates to Danish times. Make stops at the numerous labeled examples of the island's vegetation to add to your child's botanical knowledge *(see p67)*.

4 Snorkel Trunk Bay, St. John

With lifeguards on duty and underwater signs pointing out the features of its underwater trail, Trunk Bay provides easy snorkeling for novices. Kids with a bit more experience can snorkel off Trunk Cay. Rent snorkel gear near the snack stand, where you can get burgers if you haven't brought lunch *(see p11 & p63)*.

5 Coral World, St. Thomas

Coral World provides the ideal introduction to the undersea world that surrounds the Virgin Islands. With easy-to-understand exhibits, kid-friendly staff, and a nearby beach, this

Fort Christianvaern, St. Croix

A learn to dive program in progress

marine park is a must-see for visitors to St. Thomas. It's a great place to spend the entire day *(see pp18–19)*.

6 Fort Christian, St. Thomas

Kids can clang the jail cell doors, climb the stairs to the fort's ramparts, and play tag in the huge parade grounds. The small museum has some nifty artifacts for children keen on history. While the kids are letting off steam, adults can enjoy the rampart views *(see p16)*.

Atlantis Adventures

7 Atlantis Adventures, St. Thomas

Head 90 ft (27 m) down into the briny deep on this 48-passenger submarine and view colorful reefs and watch marine life swim by through large portholes. Not for the claustrophobic. The trip also includes a boat ride out to the submarine *(see p76)*.

8 Learn to Sail, All Islands

Several resorts in the USVI and BVI have children's learn to sail programs. The summer

program at the Bitter End Yacht Club in Virgin Gorda gets lots of accolades. Kids learn on small, easy-to-handle boats. They must be able to swim *(see p92)*.

9 Learn to Dive, All Islands

Kids over 10 can experience the underwater world through a basic diving course or spend more time to receive their diving certification card. Instructors are child-friendly and understand their limitations. There's no better way to add that wow factor to a USVI or BVI vacation.

10 Look for Shells, All Islands

Kids as well as adults can spend delightful hours strolling along a stretch of beach, picking up shells and exploring the water's edge as they go. Rocky and reefy beaches are good bets because they get less traffic and the tide pools are home to an interesting array of creatures.

Queen Conch Shells

Hold a queen conch shell to your ear to hear the sound of the sea. A bit romanticized, yes, but a good reason to scour USVI and BVI beaches for this prized shell. Also called pink conch after its interior color, the queen conch shell is usually found at beaches that front on bays with lots of seagrass beds to serve as shelter. Get hold of a shell book to identify the variety of shells found on tropical beaches.

For kid-friendly restaurants **See p33**

North Sound Road, Virgin Gorda

Drives & Views

1 North Shore of St. Croix
Windswept vistas greet drivers who make this out-of-the-way drive from Salt River to Davis Beach. Turn north off Route 75 onto Route 80, which runs along Salt River Bay and the North Shore. On clear days, you can see St. John to the north. The road twists and turns past old sugar mills and sprawling estates such as Rust Up Twist and La Vallee. ✪ Map C4

2 Judith's Fancy, St. Croix
Splendid views of Salt River and the sea, plus a stroll through plantation ruins dating to around 1750 (see p9), reward motorists who drive through this gated neighborhood of upscale homes. Just check in with the guard first. Follow Hamilton Avenue to the end for glimpses of Salt River Bay. Turn off onto Caribe Drive to see the ruins, which include those of a great house

and a tower. This is a small neighborhood, so don't worry about getting lost. ✪ Map C4

3 Ham's Bluff Road, St. Croix
Running north from just outside Frederiksted to the end of the paved road, this appealing drive (Route 63) takes you past gracious old homes and to the west, magnificent sea views. If you're up for a dirt-road drive, connect with Scenic Road (see p59) near the end of the drive. ✪ Map A4

4 North Shore of St. John
If you only do one thing on St. John, make it this drive from the outskirts of Cruz Bay to Annaberg along the North Shore Road (Route 20). Stunning vistas of white beaches and turquoise seas unfold at Caneel Bay, Trunk Bay, and Maho Bay overlooks. A part of the BVI chain of islands is visible to the north ✪ Map D2

North Shore of St. John

The restaurant at Bordeaux Overlook

5 Bordeaux Overlook, St. John

Stop at this busy overlook for gorgeous views of the sea, Coral Bay, and in the distance, the BVI. There's a tiny gift shop where you can buy some interesting souvenirs to take home. A snack shop and restaurant make this a good break on your round-the-island tour (see p65).

6 Centerline Road Overlook toward Whistling Cay, St. John

As you head from Cruz Bay toward Coral Bay, take time to stop at this small overlook midway between Catherineburg Ruins (see p65) and Bordeaux Overlook. A National Park sign points out the features spread out before you. ◈ Map E2

7 Drake's Seat, St. Thomas

Stellar panoramic views of Magens Bay and the BVI highlight this overlook. According to legend, the 16th-century explorer Sir Francis Drake kept watch on his fleet from this spot.

A seat on the inland side of the overlook commemorates this event (see p74).

8 Ridge Route, St. Thomas

With a map in hand, drive this route for lovely sea views to the north and a glimpse of some of St. Thomas's luxurious homes. Start at Crown Mountain, following Route 40 east, through Estate Elizabeth and Wintberg to Route 42, ending at Tabor and Harmony. The route passes through small communities along the way. It's easy to get lost – just stop and ask directions if you do. ◈ Map B2

9 North Coast/Ridge Road, Tortola

Rural Tortola reveals itself as you make your way from Long Bay to Long Look along this road. Goats and cows wander at will as you pass villages such as Carrot Bay and Cane Garden Bay, historic ruins, and breathtaking sea views. Beachfront restaurants along the route make nice stops for lunch or drinks. ◈ Map G5

10 North Sound Road, Virgin Gorda

Take this route along Virgin Gorda's spine from Savannah Bay to North Sound for spectacular ocean and beach views. You can make a stop along the way for a swim or walk where you might just be the only visitor. There are no services until you reach North Sound. ◈ Map L3

Left **View from Drake's Seat, St. Thomas** Right **North Coast Road, Tortola**

Drive carefully – most of the islands' roads are narrow and winding and traffic is impatient. See also p97

Left **Gallery Gia, St. Croix** Right **Coconut Coast Studios, St. John**

Art Galleries

1 Maria Henle Studio, St. Croix

Using a process called color etchings as well as oils, Maria Henle creates stunning works that often reflect the sea. She applies various views of a subject to create pictures within pictures. Henle also exhibits the works of her father, famed St. Croix photographer Fritz Henle, in the gallery. ✎ Map D5 • 55 Company St, Christiansted • 340-773-7376 • www.mariahenlestudio.com

2 Gallery Gia, St. Croix

Appealingly set in an old town house, Gallery Gia showcases the pastels and oils of St. Croix artist Deborah Broad. It also exhibits paintings, photography, etchings, sculpture, and wood carvings by artists from around the Caribbean. ✎ Map D5 • 5A King St, Christiansted • 340-713-9880 • www.gallerygia.com

3 Bajo El Sol, St. John

Long-time St. John residents Aimee Trayser and Les Anderson exhibit their own works as well as those of others here. Both artists capture Caribbean hues and sights with their own particular flair. There's also a good selection of sculpture, jewelry, and wood pieces. ✎ Map D2 • Mongoose Junction Shopping Center, North Shore Rd (Rte 20), Cruz Bay • 340-693-7070 • www.bajoelsolgallery.com

4 Solo Arté, St. John

Janet Cook Rutnik exhibits her varied works and those of others at this lovely gallery in the nether reaches of a ramshackle shopping area. Her works are often dark with splashes of color, very different from most other Caribbean art. ✎ Map D2 • Lumberyard Shopping Complex, Boulon Center Rd, Cruz Bay • 340-715-2150

5 Coconut Coast Studios, St. John

Owner Elaine Estern's pieces, inspired by the life just offshore her seaside gallery, reflect the colors of the Caribbean and often feature her dog, M&M. Estern's shop carries original works as well as prints, note cards, and more. ✎ Map D2 • Off Rte 105, Frank Bay, outside Cruz Bay • 340-776-6944 • www.coconutcoaststudios.com

6 Gallery St. Thomas

This gallery displays works by many island artists, including Lucinda Schutt's island scenes and Avelino Samuel's turned wood pieces. Most works focus

Painting by Janet Cook Rutnik, Solo Arté, St. John

on the Caribbean, but some surprises await those who visit this spacious gallery housed in a historic building. ◈ *Map P2 • Garden St, Charlotte Amalie, St. Thomas • 340-774-9440 • www.gallerystthomas.com*

7 MaPes Monde, St. Thomas
Owner Michael Paiewonsky has gathered a huge collection of old maps, books, prints by such notables as Camille Pissarro, and other unusual pieces. MaPes Monde also has a branch at the Marketplace Shopping Center in St. John. ◈ *Map P2; Grand Hotel at Post Office Sq, Charlotte Amalie; 340-776-2160 • Map N2; A.H. Riise on Main St, Charlotte Amalie; 340-776-2886*

8 Camille Pissarro Gallery, St. Thomas
Located on the second floor of the house where acclaimed Impressionist painter Camille Pissarro was born, this gallery features works by island artists working in a variety of mediums, but not by Pissarro. His works are on display at Government House *(see p17)*. ◈ *Map N2 • 14 Main St, Charlotte Amalie • 340-774-4621*

9 Mango Tango, St. Thomas
The island's best artists exhibit at this gallery, tucked away at the back of a shopping center. The large selection of fine take-home gifts includes cigars and soap. ◈ *Map C2 • Al Cohen's Plaza, Raphune Hill, Weymouth Rhymer Hwy (Rte 38) • 340-777-3060*

10 Sunny Caribbee Gallery, Tortola
Selections include lithographs of modern Tortola, prints of old maps, metal works, and brightly colored paintings that will remind you of the tropics long after your vacation is over. ◈ *Map H4 • Main St, Road Town • 284-494-2178*

Top 10 Made in the Islands

1 Sonya's, St. Croix
The swirls on the clasp of her hook bracelets commemorate hurricanes that have ravaged the islands. ◈ *Map D5 • Christiansted • 340-778-8605*

2 St. John Glassworks, St. John
Nifty recycled glass items. ◈ *Map D2 • Cruz Bay • 340-693-9544*

3 Donald Schnell Studio, St. John
Quality pottery with island motifs. ◈ *Map D2 • Cruz Bay • 340-776-6420*

4 Awl Made Here, St. John
Handcrafted leather goods are the highlights. ◈ *Map F2 • Coral Bay • 340-777-5757*

5 Native Arts & Crafts Cooperative, St. Thomas
Stunning quilts. ◈ *Map P3 • Charlotte Amalie • 340-777-1153*

6 Zora's Sandals, St. Thomas
Comfortable, custom-fitted leather sandals. ◈ *Map P2 • Charlotte Amalie • 340-774-2559*

7 Kilnworks Pottery, St. Thomas
Elegant pottery and a large array of crafts. ◈ *Map C2 • Smith Bay • 340-775-3979*

8 Bamboushay, Tortola
Exquisite pottery inspired by the sea. ◈ *Map H5 • Nanny Cay • 284-494-0393*

9 Crafts Alive Market, Tortola
The island's best artisans set up shop at this Road Town market. ◈ *Map H4*

10 Pat's Pottery, Anegada
Bright hand-thrown pottery. ◈ *Map L2 • Near the Settlement • 284-495-8031*

Left **St. Croix Christmas Festival** Right **July 4th Celebration, St. John**

Festivals & Events

1 St. Croix Christmas Festival

Lasting through December until Three Kings Day, this annual festival features a plethora of events, from parades to musical programs. Sample island dishes at Food Fair, held in mid-December. Event locations vary, usually between Christiansted and Frederiksted in alternating years.
◊ 340-719-3379

2 Agrifest, St. Croix

This mega event, held every February at the Agriculture Department Grounds, puts a new spin on the country fair. Look for agricultural exhibits as well as games, food, old-time music, and cooking demonstrations. St. Croix's youthful members of the international group 4-H also put on displays at the Agrifest. ◊ Map B5 • Off Centerline Rd (Rte 70), Upper Love • 340-692-4080

3 July 4th Celebration, St. John

This annual June and July event wraps up with a three-hour parade through the streets of Cruz Bay. The music is deafening, the town overflowing, and the fun on the party-hearty side. You won't see much in the way of American flags; this is definitely a Caribbean event.
◊ Map D2 • 340-693-8036

4 St. Thomas Carnival

Held every April, sometimes running into May, this event, like those on the other islands, has numerous activities including parades, beauty pageants, and food fairs. The closing parade is an all-day affair that draws thousands to Main Street in Charlotte Amalie. ◊ Map N2 • 340-775-1320 • www.vicarnival.com

5 Agricultural Fair, St. Thomas

While the locals shop for plants, herbs, and fresh veggies at this November fair, savvy visitors look for well-made crafts seldom seen in shops. Handcrafted dolls and small brooms made of palm fronds make unusual take-home gifts. ◊ Map B2 • University of the Virgin Islands, Brewers Bay Rd (Rte 30), Brewers Bay • 340-693-1080

6 Texas Society's Chili Cookoff, St. Thomas

Texas meets the Caribbean at this annual September event held at Bolongo Bay Beach

St. Thomas Carnival Parade

Club (see p115). Island chefs cook up vats of mouth-watering chili to vie for top honors. The music is loud, but the crowd congenial. ⊗ Map C2 • Bovoni Rd, Bovoni • 340-775-8011

7 August Monday Festival, Tortola
Commemorating the end of slavery on August 1, 1834, Tortola's carnival is marked by a day-long parade in Road Town, athletic events, beauty pageants, and food fairs. Even in a region not known for punctuality, the parade is notorious for hours-late starts. ⊗ Map H4 • 284-494-3701

8 Agricultural Fair, Tortola
This week-long event in February or early March features a produce and livestock exhibition by farmers at H. Lavity Stoutt Community College. Additional exhibitions are held across the territory. The finale is a food fair where you can savor island fare. ⊗ Map J4 • Off Blackburn Hwy, Paraquita Bay • 284-495-2110

9 Virgin Gorda Easter Festival
The island shifts into party mode every Easter weekend for its annual carnival. A beauty pageant and a small parade are the highlights. Residents of other islands often visit at this time, so make hotel bookings early. ⊗ Map L4 • Spanish Town • 284-495-5181

10 Foxy's Wooden Boat Regatta, Jost Van Dyke
This exciting boat race, to Cane Garden Bay in Tortola and back, held the last weekend in May, attracts skippers of all manner of wooden boats. The legendary beach parties are full of food, fun, and music. ⊗ Map G3 • Great Harbour • 284-494-9262

Top 10 Musical Events

1 St. Croix Landmarks Society's Candlelight Concert Series
The Whim Plantation Museum hosts fine concerts in winter. ⊗ Map B6 • 340-772-0598

2 Jazz Vespers, St. Croix
Good jazz, at the St. Croix Reformed Church in La Reine. ⊗ Map C5 • 340-778-0520

3 St. John School of the Arts Performances
Touring performers in winter at this tiny Cruz Bay theater. ⊗ Map D2 • 340-779-4322

4 St. John Singers Christmas Concerts
Concerts in Cruz and Coral Bay churches. ⊗ Map D2, F2

5 Challenge of the Carols, St. Thomas
Amateur groups perform early Christmas morning in Emancipation Garden. ⊗ Map P3 • 340-774-6361

6 Pistarkle Theater Performances, St. Thomas
Amateur shows, Tillet Gardens. ⊗ Map C2 • 340-775-7877

7 Tillett Gardens Performances, St. Thomas
Classics, blues, and jazz. ⊗ Map C2 • 340-775-1929

8 Reichhold Center for the Arts, St. Thomas
Classical ballet through to hot pop at the University of the VI arena. ⊗ Map B2 • 340-693-1559

9 BVI Music Festival, Tortola
Reggae, gospel, blues, and salsa at Cane Garden Bay in May. ⊗ Map G4 • 284-494-3134

10 H. Lavity Stoutt Community College Classics in the Atrium Concerts, Tortola
The annual concert series runs from October to May. ⊗ Map J4 • 284-494-4994

Left **Bike ride at the Love City Triathlon, St. John** Right **Carnival Parade, St. Thomas**

ᴛᴏᴘ10 Places to Mingle with Locals

1 Ruins Rambles, St. Croix
Join St. Croix Landmarks Society members on their monthly rambles through the many ruins that dot the island. The easy 1- to 2-hour guided walks run November through May. Members finish the day with a wine and cheese party. You need to book in advance. ✆ 304-772-0598 • www.stcroixlandmarks.com • Adm

2 Starving Artist Days, St. Croix
In March, August, and November, the St. Croix Landmarks Society sponsors an arts and crafts fair at Whim Plantation Museum *(see p58)*. Music, food, and camaraderie round off the day. This event affords an opportunity to explore the St. Croix art scene as well as sample local culture. ✆ Map B6 • Centerline Rd (Rte 70) • 340-772-0598 • www.stcroixlandmarks.com

3 8 Tuff Miles Race, St. John
Several hundred people make the 8.375-mile (13-km) trip up hill and down dale from Cruz Bay to Coral Bay on a Saturday in late February. This race attracts top-notch runners, walkers, and even a couple of people pushing baby carriages. The course record

8 Tuff Miles Race, St. John

stands at 53:15. ✆ Map D2 • 340-779-4035 • www.8tuffmiles.com

4 Love City Triathlon, St. John
A half-mile (1-km) swim, 14-mile (22-km) bike ride up and downhill from Maho Bay to Cruz Bay and on to Coral Bay plus a 4-mile (6-km) run mark this annual early September event, held at Maho Bay and in Coral Bay. A good spectator event. ✆ Map E2 • 340-776-6226

5 Transfer Day Celebration, St. Thomas
The who's who of St. Thomas society gathers every March 31 to remember the 1917 event that transferred ownership of the islands from Denmark to the US. The venue is the Legislature Building on the waterfront, the same site as that of the original transfer ceremony. ✆ Map P3 • Veterans Dr (Rte 30), Charlotte Amalie

6 Carnival Parade, St. Thomas
Lifelong friendships between islanders and visitors can begin when they share a patch of sidewalk at the annual April Carnival parade. It's easy to strike up a conversation by asking polite questions. The day-long parade

features colorful floats, troupes, and floupes, which are floats with troupes parading behind.
Ⓢ *Map N2 • Main St, Charlotte Amalie*
• 340-775-1320 • www.vicarnival.com

7 Queen's Birthday Celebration, Tortola & Virgin Gorda

Like their counterparts across the British Commonwealth, BVIers celebrate the Queen's birthday every June. Filled with pageantry, the event brings out the cream of BVI society as well as school groups and bands. The governor reads a message from the Queen and hands out awards. Ⓢ *Map H4; A.O. Shirley Recreation Grounds, Off Waterfront Dr, Road Town • Map L4; VG Recreation Grounds, Spanish Town; 284-494-3701*

8 Happy Hours at Many Bars, All Islands

Most bars hold happy hours in the late afternoon, with the free munchies attracting locals, particularly on Fridays. If you want to learn more about local life from the horse's mouth, here's your chance.

9 Art Receptions, All Islands

Meet the islands' art communities at monthly gallery receptions. A great opportunity to enjoy the latest from the local artists as well as sip a glass of free wine and sample the cheese tray. The daily newspapers list the latest art happenings.

10 Full Moon Parties, All Islands

An island tradition at local restaurants and bars, full moon parties run the gamut from full-scale blowouts with ear-splitting music and huge crowds to more sedate affairs with jazz and special menus.

Top 10 Local Words & Expressions

1 All mash up
Broken. Your vehicle gets *all mash up* when you hit a wrong-side-of-the-road tourist who forgot to drive on the left.

2 Bahn har
Born here. Virgin Islanders, particularly those *bahn har*, put great stock in where they were born.

3 Bush
The woods or any place outside of developed areas. He *gone bush* means he has disappeared.

4 Jeese and bread!
A benign swear word or exclamation. *Jeese and bread*, it sure is hot today!

5 For true?
Really? This is a response to a questionable statement. It's gunna rain. *For true?*

6 Gut
A gully or ravine. In heavy rains, water from the hillsides rushes down *guts* to the sea.

7 Limin'
Hanging out. When you go out on Friday nights, you don't go anywhere special. You're going *limin'*.

8 Meh son
A generic phrase inserted in sentences. I had to walk miles, *meh son*, and it was very tough.

9 Melee
Gossip or rumor. The rumor mills run overtime in the islands, with residents taking to radio talk shows to air the latest *melee*.

10 Walk with
Take. Don't forget to *walk with* your passport or other identification when visiting the islands.

Virgin Islands' Top 10

Left **Purchase of the US Virgin Islands, 1917** Right **Transfer of Danish colonies to the US, 1917**

🔟 Moments in History

1 Christopher Columbus Arrives in USVI & BVI
Sailing through in 1493 on his second trip to the New World, Columbus stopped at Salt River, St. Croix, to skirmish with the Carib Indians. The many islands he saw prompted him to name the archipelago after St. Ursula and the 11,000 Virgins.

2 Slave Rebellion in 1733, St. John
In their first attempt to gain freedom, slaves used cane knives to attack the Danish garrison at Coral Bay. They subsequently held the island's planters hostage for six months, killing many of them. The siege ended with help from French soldiers based in Martinique.

1801 letter of freedom for a St. Croix slave before Emancipation was declared in 1848

3 Emancipation, BVI
After Great Britain set the stage by outlawing slavery in 1808 and then seized a number of slave-carrying ships in BVI waters, this British colony finally freed its slaves on August 1, 1834. The former slaves continued life as paid laborers.

4 Emancipation, USVI
Rioting slaves marched on Frederiksted, St. Croix, in 1848, forcing Danish Governor Peter Von Scholten to declare from the ramparts of Fort Frederik that "All unfree in the Danish West Indies are from today emancipated." His decree also included St. Thomas and St. John.

5 Earthquake
While the region witnesses frequent minor earthquakes, none were as disastrous as the one that hit in November 18, 1867. A huge tsunami emptied the harbor in Charlotte Amalie, St. Thomas, leaving fish lying on the ocean floor, and then surged back, killing many people who had gone out to collect the fish.

6 Fireburn, St. Croix
Years of poor crops, hurricanes, and other calamities pushed agricultural laborers to the brink, leading to the October 1, 1878 Fireburn. Frederiksted and other parts of St. Croix went up in flames on the only day of the year laborers were allowed to sign new work contracts.

The USVI observes Transfer Day every year with ceremonies at the Legislature in St. Thomas

7 Transfer of Danish Colonies to US

After years of negotiations, Denmark sold St. Thomas, St. John, and St. Croix to the US for $25 million. The Danish flag came down to make way for the Stars and Stripes on March 31, 1917.

8 Virgin Islands National Park Opens

Laurance Rockefeller bought up many acres of St. John land and donated them to the federal government in an act of foresight that has helped preserve St. John's natural environment. The park, and Rockefeller's posh Caneel Bay Resort (see p112), opened December 1, 1956.

9 Royalty Visits the BVI

Queen Elizabeth and Prince Philip visited Tortola on February 23, 1966 and again on October 26, 1977, riding in a motorcade through the island's streets. The late Princess Margaret visited on March 8, 1972.

10 Disastrous Hurricanes Hit USVI & BVI

Both territories suffered massive devastation when Hurricane Hugo hit on September 17 and 18, 1989 and Marilyn on September 15 and 16, 1995. Other hurricanes in the late 1990s caused further damage, prompting strengthening of the infrastructure against future catastrophes.

Hurricane Marilyn's impact on St Thomas

Top 10 Virgin Islanders

1 Alexander Hamilton, St. Croix

Born in Nevis but raised in St. Croix, Hamilton became the first secretary of the US Treasury in 1789.

2 Bennie Benjamin, St. Croix

The St. Croix-born Benjamin co-authored the 1952 musical hit, "Wheel of Fortune."

3 Tim Duncan, St. Croix

Born April 25, 1976, the St. Croix native plays basketball for the San Antonio Spurs.

4 Peter Holmberg, St. Thomas

Silver medalist in sailing (Finn class) at the 1988 Olympics.

5 Emile Griffith, St. Thomas

This fighter born in 1938 holds professional boxing titles.

6 Elrod Hendricks, St. Thomas

Played baseball, mainly for the Baltimore Orioles (1968–79).

7 Camille Pissarro, St. Thomas

A major French Impressionist painter, Pissarro (1830–1903) was born in St. Thomas.

8 Richard Humphreys, Tortola

A Tortola-born Quaker, Richard Humphreys' 1837 bequest of $10,000 funded the US's first black college, now Cheney University in Pennsylvania.

9 Samuel Hodge, Tortola

The first black man to receive Britain's Victoria Cross, this Tortola native fought in the 1866 Ashanti wars.

10 William Thornton, Jost Van Dyke

The Jost Van Dyke-born Thornton designed the US Capitol building in 1792–93.

Left **Bananaquit** Center **Donkeys in Coral Bay, St. John** Right **Iguana**

🔟 Animals & Birds

1 Bananaquits
So small they would fit in your hand, these tiny yellow birds dart in for a quick taste of sugar or flower nectar. They're also known as sugar birds and yellow breasts. If you listen closely, you can hear them chirp.

2 Donkeys
Used as transportation until cars became commonplace in the 1950s, the ubiquitous donkeys now roam island by-ways. The largest population lives in St. John's Virgin Islands National Park and its environs. Their braying can keep you awake at night. Don't get up close and personal with them; they can deliver a mean kick.

3 Iguanas
Looking like prehistoric creatures, bright green baby iguanas and the darker adults thrive all over the US and British Virgin Islands, but trees in dry areas see greater populations. They're somewhat elusive in most areas, and a sighting is a special event.

4 Goats
Eaten by residents in a variety of dishes, goats roam where they want in the St. John's Coral Bay area and throughout the BVI. Their eating habits cause extensive erosion problems and their droppings make paths slippery. They're also noisy creatures, particularly when a baby goes astray.

5 Herons
Several varieties of herons are found all over the Virgin Islands. Look for little blue herons, West Indian green herons, and rarely, great blue herons, near the shorelines. Their nests sit on shrubby trees and are made of sticks.

Hummingbird

6 Hummingbirds

With wings flapping at phenomenal speeds, hummingbirds hover over flowers to dine on their nectar. Mostly green in color, they're easy to spot as they dart here and there. They're so well loved that residents make homes for them in feeders made of coconut shells.

7 Migrating Birds

The USVI and BVI sit in the flyway for migrating birds heading south for the winter from the US mainland. So many arrive that the Audubon Society and private groups conduct annual Christmas bird counts on several islands.

8 Mongoose

Originally imported to control rats, mongooses are now well settled in the islands. You'll see these long, brown, and furry animals scurrying across the road or poking around garbage cans. Mongoose Junction Shopping Center in St. John is so named because the creatures gathered at garbage cans located nearby.

9 Pearly-Eyed Thrashers

Called trushies by locals, these common brown birds will make moves on your picnic lunch if you're not careful. You'll hear them craw-crawing all over the islands. They're particularly prevalent at beaches where people carelessly discard food.

10 Pelicans

With a big splash, these broad-billed brown sea birds dive under the water's edge for a fish dinner. Watch out if you're snorkeling over schools of small fish. They seldom crashland on snorkelers' heads, but when they hit the water, the noise can give you a good scare.

Top 10 Undersea Creatures

1 Blue Tang

Schools of this small, round, deep blue fish swim near reefs and rocks. Fun to watch while snorkeling.

2 Conch

This mollusk lives in seagrass beds. If you find an empty shell on the beach, hold it to your ear to hear the sea.

3 Dolphin

Dolphins usually live in deeper water, so look for them a bit offshore as they arc in and out.

4 Whales

If you're visiting in the spring, watch for whales cavorting offshore on your day sail or fishing trip.

5 Lobster

It takes good eyes to spot this crustacean poking its antennae out of its hidey hole on the reef.

6 Sea Cucumbers

Looking a lot like their namesake vegetable, sea cucumbers slink along the ocean floor as they feed.

7 Spiny Sea Urchins

Black with long, protruding spines, these undersea creatures live on the reef.

8 Starfish

Look along the ocean floor for yellow-gold starfish. They're not that common, so it's a real treat to find them.

9 Tarpon

Large, silvery tarpon swim near schools of baby fish, called fry. They're harmless, despite their size.

10 Barracuda

Teeth bared, this long, slim fish looks like it's waiting to attack, but it will ignore you if you don't bother it.

Left **Bougainvillea** Center **Hibiscus** Right **Allamanda**

TOP 10 Plants

1 Air Plants
These plants, officially called epiphytes, drip from the crooks of trees all over the islands. The long, thin leaves sprout from a center that looks slightly like that of a pineapple. Air plants get their sustenance from decomposing leaf matter caught in their leaves and moisture from the air.

2 Allamanda
This lush green plant carries a yellow trumpet-shaped flower, leading to its other name, golden trumpet. The leaves are thick, smooth, and pointy and its milky sap is poisonous. Popular with landscapers and home gardeners, the plant usually grows in vines or hedges.

3 Anthurium
This unusual flower is one of the islands' loveliest. Its waxy, heart-shaped flower comes in shades of pink, white, or red. A tapered shoot protrudes from the center. While anthurium grow in the wild, you can buy them as cut flowers from stalls by the roadside.

4 Bougainvillea
In colors that range from basic magenta to every spectrum of the red, orange, and white family, this Caribbean staple decorates yards and gardens across the islands. The plants can grow to an enormous size, but most serve as hedges.

5 Bird of Paradise
These exotic and flamboyant flowers look like bright red or orange birds sitting on deep green leaves. You'll find them mainly in well-tended gardens, but in some moist places, they grow in the wild.

6 Hibiscus
The workhorse of Caribbean gardens and roadsides, this shrub bears flowers in myriad hues. Red is the most common, but there are literally thousands of varieties with single, double, and even triple blooms. Picked blooms stay open all day.

7 Night-Blooming Cereus
When night falls during the summer months, the waxy white flowers of this cactus-like plant give off an exquisite sweet aroma. The large, showy flowers are simply lovely to watch as they open at dusk. After they close the next morning, the flowers develop into tasty fruits.

8 Oleander
Gardeners all over the islands usually prune the pink- or white-flowered oleander into rows as a hedge. The wood is

Anthurium

Oleander

poisonous to animals so folks often plant them near more fragile plants to keep foraging goats and donkeys away.

9 Spider Lily
Most of the year, spider lilies look like rather pedestrian green-leafed plants growing along the roadside, but summer sees them burst into bloom all over the islands with a shower of white flowers. If you are very patient, you can watch them open at dusk. The lilies last only a few days before drying up.

10 Ixora
With large, rounded scarlet blooms made up of individual flowers and set on green leaves, ixora looks somewhat like a geranium. This year-round bloomer is popular with home gardeners and landscapers who use it as a hedge.

Ixora

Top 10 Trees

1 Bay Rum Tree
Fragrant bay rum trees grow in woody areas. The leaves are often used to make aftershave.

2 Broom Palm
The only indigenous palm, this short tree has thin fronds that form a larger circular leaf.

3 Calabash
Artisans use the gourd-like fruit to make bowls and musical instruments. It grows quite tall in forested areas.

4 Flamboyant
Come summer, bright red and orange flamboyants bloom all over the islands. You may also see a gold variety.

5 Ginger Thomas
This tree grows in such profusion on hillsides and roadways that its yellow blossom serves as the USVI territorial flower.

6 Lime Tree
Bearing yellow-green fruits used in everything from ice tea to tarts, lime trees grow wild and in gardens.

7 Mahogany
Stretching skyward, stately mahogany trees grow mostly in parks. Craftspeople use its wood to make furniture.

8 Manchineel
Watch out for this tree found near beaches. It bears poisonous red fruits and the sap is extremely toxic.

9 Palms
From tall coconut-bearing trees to shorter feathery varieties, palm trees are found all over the USVI and BVI.

10 Turpentine Tree
Residents call them tourist trees because their bark is red and peels. These tall trees grow all over the islands.

Find native and exotic plants in profusion at St. George Village Botanical Garden **See p58**

AROUND THE VIRGIN ISLANDS

VIRGIN ISLANDS' TOP TEN

Left **Sea view from Fort Christianvaern** Center **Steeple Building** Right **Point Udall**

St. Croix

AN ISLAND OF CONTRASTS, *St. Croix* combines a rural feel with excellent dining choices, great golf courses, and airport access. Beachfront resorts of all sizes, a handful of small hotels tucked away in the island's two towns, numerous condominium complexes on the beach and up in the hills, old sugar plantation ruins, and an oil refinery all share its 58 sq miles (150 sq km) of rolling hills and undulating coastline. Its size makes it large enough for some interesting drives, but small enough to find the perfect patch of island sun. In short, St. Croix combines the best of the other USVI islands sitting 40 miles (64 km) to the north, with a pace not as slow as St. John's but with less bustle than St. Thomas.

Old Custom House, Christiansted

🔟 Sights

1. Christiansted
2. Point Udall
3. Sunny Isle
4. Cruzan Rum Distillery
5. St. George Village Botanical Garden
6. Whim Plantation Museum
7. Frederiksted
8. Carl & Marie Lawaetz Museum
9. Scenic Road
10. Salt River Bay National Historic Park & Ecological Preserve

Previous pages **Aerial view of St. Thomas**

Christiansted

Isaac Bays starts off from near the parking lot. The bays' inaccessibility makes them safe for hikers who worry about undesirable elements lurking at the next bend in the trail. ✎ *Map F4 • Off Rte 82*

1 Christiansted

History and commerce come together in this charming town. Historic Fort Christianvaern casts its shadow over Christiansted National Historic Site, but the past permeates the entire town *(see p8)*. Stroll by pastel buildings dating from the 18th and 19th centuries, then segue off to a delightful lunch at a fine or casual restaurant. Small shops with eclectic merchandise offer an afternoon's diversion. ✎ *Map D4 • Christiansted Nat. Historic Site, Hospital St • 340-773-1460 • www.nps. gov/chri • Hrs vary by building, but usually 9am–4:30pm daily • Adm to Steeple Building & Fort Christianvaern*

2 Point Udall

The sun rises first over the US at Point Udall, the easternmost point in St. Croix. While windswept vistas are the reason to go, the area also features a monument erected for the 2000 Millennium celebration. A downhill hike to the remote Jack and

Hovensa

Unlike St. John and St. Thomas, St. Croix does not rely solely on tourism for its economy. The huge Hovensa refinery directly employs more than 1,000 people. Its contract work force adds hundreds more, making it the largest employer in the USVI. Built in 1966, the refinery is off Melvin Evans Highway (Route 66).

3 Sunny Isle

With a shopping center that's home to a Kmart department store, grocery stores, movie theaters, and fast food places, Sunny Isle and its environs are the heart of the island's economy. Go there for a gander at island life. Visitors find it a great place to shop for incidentals at better prices than in hotel or in-town shops, and it's a convenient lunch stop on your drive from Christiansted to Frederiksted. ✎ *Map C5 • Centerline Rd (Rte 70)*

Cruzan Rum Distillery

4 Cruzan Rum Distillery

A stop at the Cruzan Rum Distillery gives you a glimpse into the island's rum-based history as well as the present. The distillery, now owned by a liquor conglomerate and using modern methods, still has enough old buildings to make it a worthwhile visit. Your tour through the rum-making process ends with a free rum tasting; you can also shop for rum *(see p35)*, rum cakes, and t-shirts at its store. ✎ *Map B5 • West Airport Rd, Estate Diamond • 340-692-2280 • Adm*

Fort Frederiksted

5 St. George Village Botanical Garden

Built on the ruins of a 19th-century plantation, this lovely 17-acre spot features more than 1,500 native and exotic species of plants, including 60 stunning orchid species. Even if you're not into botany, the plants are beautiful to look at and the location tranquil. Those keen on history will enjoy exploring the workers' village, factory, and other buildings standing since sugarcane grew in the surrounding fields. ✪ Map B5 • Off Centerline Rd (Rte 70), turn north at the sign for St. George Estate • 340-692-2874 • www.sgvbg.org • 9am–5pm daily • Adm

6 Whim Plantation Museum

The showpiece of the island's plantation history, Whim Plantation Museum (see p9) typifies plantations established by the Danish West Indian Company in the 1730s. Planters first grew cotton, but records show that by 1754 sugar was the main crop, a status it enjoyed until the 1920s. Refurbished by the St. Croix Landmarks Society, the plantation has an oval great house full of antiques. The outbuildings

Windmill, Whim Plantation

spread over its 12 acres include a windmill, sugar factory, and kitchen. Sugarcane still grows in nearby fields. ✪ Map B6 • Centerline Rd (Rte 70) • 340-772-0598 • Open 10am–4pm Mon, Wed, Fri & Sat • Adm

7 Frederiksted

St. Croix's second town, Frederiksted (see p9) is more like a sleepy village that seems to come alive only when a rare cruise ship pulls up to the pier. That makes its waterfront Strand Street and the few other streets ideal for strolling. The huge Fort Frederik is a good place to start. It has a few exhibits and the usual guns, but it is also home to the quirky Virgin Islands Police Museum. The park out front is a good spot for a break. ✪ Map A5 • Fort open 8:30am–4:30pm Mon–Fri

8 Carl & Marie Lawaetz Museum

Take a trip back in time to the Lawaetz family estate (see p9) in Little LaGrange, managed by the St. Croix Landmarks Society with Lawaetz family members often serving as tour guides. Carl Lawaetz, originally from Denmark, bought the property in 1896 after serving six years as its overseer. Marie arrived from Denmark in 1902 after Carl courted her long distance. Their gardens and furnishings, now

---

Slavery & its Legacy

Much of St. Croix's history, like that of other Caribbean Islands, is based on slavery. Captured in Africa, the slaves were transported across the Atlantic to work on St. Croix's 100 or so plantations. While this profane practice ended when slaves rioted to gain their freedom on July 3, 1848, the windmills built during this era still dot the island's countryside.

antiques, remain to remind visitors of another era. ◈ Map B5 • Rte 76, Little LaGrange • 340-772-1539 • www.stcroixlandmarks.com • Open 10am–3pm Tue, Thu & Sat • Adm

9 Scenic Road

Leading uphill along the island's ridge, Scenic Road (Route 78) runs east–west from Route 80 near Salt River to Ham's Bluff Road outside Frederiksted. It intersects paved roads several times, so you don't have to make the entire 8-or-so-mile (13 km) of this mostly dirt road. Rent a vehicle with four-wheel drive and high clearance to navigate Scenic Road. You'll find no development along this route, just forest flora and fauna with an occasional fine view. The solitude is stunning.

10 Salt River Bay National Historic Park & Ecological Preserve

Undeveloped, this 948-acre seaside park is where Christopher Columbus sent a party ashore to look for fresh water on his second trip through the New World in 1493 (see p48). A skirmish with the Carib Indians resulted, with Columbus's men getting the worst of it. It takes some sleuthing to ferret out more history – a small hill on the eastern side of the parking area is what remains of an old Dutch earth fort. ◈ Map C4 • Off Rte 80 • 340-773-1460

Carl & Marie Lawaetz Museum

An Easy Day

Morning

🕐 Get up early to watch the sun rise at **Point Udall**, at the island's easternmost tip. Sunrise varies by season, so check with your hotel's front desk to find out what time to depart. After snapping a few photos of the sun peeking over the horizon, head west to the **Buccaneer Hotel**'s (see p112) attractive dining room for its scrumptious breakfast served buffet style and the fabulous sea views.

The point of a St. Croix vacation is not to shop till you drop or tour till you're bored, but rather to see the sights at a slow pace and spend some time in a chaise. So after breakfast, head back to your hotel for a few hours at the beach. Don't forget the sunscreen. When the sun gets high in the sky, head off to Christiansted for lunch at **Café Christine** (see p61), where you can sit in blissful shade at the alfresco porch tables.

Afternoon

Walk off your lunch with a stroll around **Christiansted**, stopping at its small shops and taking in the town's historic ambience. A halt at **Christiansted National Historic Site** (see p8) will help you understand the island's history.

Pause for a few moments at one of the benches strategically placed along the waterfront boardwalk to enjoy the sea view.

Wrap up your afternoon with a sunset sail from the Christiansted waterfront, or simply return to your hotel for a nap.

Left **Day sail to Buck Island Reef National Monument** Right **The Buccaneer Hotel golf course**

TOP 10 Outdoor Activities

1 Day Sails to Buck Island Reef National Monument

Charter boats leave from Green Cay Marina and the Christiansted waterfront for day trips to this marine park. Includes snorkeling and a few hours anchored off a fine white sand beach. *Map E4*

2 Fishing

Fish for the big ones on a saltwater trip off St. Croix on a charter boat.

3 Golf

Carambola Golf Club's 18-hole course is the best, but the 18 holes at the Buccaneer Hotel *(see p112)* also get accolades. Reef Golf Club has a nine-hole course. *Map B5; Carambola, off River Rd (Rte 69), River • Map E4; Reef Golf Club, off East End Rd (Rte 82)*

4 Hikes

While you can strike out on your own, the St. Croix Environmental Association organizes guided eco-tours through plantation ruins and natural areas. *340-773-1989 • www.seastx.org*

5 Horseback Riding

Paul and Jill's Equestrian Stables offer rides through the rainforest and the hills surrounding its base at the 18th-century Sprat Hall plantation. *Map A5 • Creque Dam Rd (Rte 58), outside Frederiksted • 340-772-2880 • Payment by cash or traveler's check*

6 Kayaking

Virgin Kayak at Cane Bay and Caribbean Adventure Tours at Salt River rent kayaks and do tours. *Map B4; Virgin Kayak, North Shore Road (Rte 80); 340-778-0071 • Map C4; Caribbean Adventure Tours, Anchor Dive Center, Rte 80; 340-778-1522*

7 Scuba

Dive sites range from patchy reefs to deep walls and canyons, and there's no shortage of dive operators to take you out.

8 Snorkeling

Rent equipment from watersports centers and shops for undersea exploration.

9 Tennis

Many hotels have their own courts, but the public is usually welcome for a small fee.

10 Windsurfing

Constant trade winds make it a breeze to windsurf Christiansted Harbor. St. Croix Watersports, a short ferry hop away from the waterfront, rents surf boards. *Map D4 • Hotel on the Cay • 340-773-7060*

Tennis court at the Buccaneer Hotel

On all the islands, your hotel can usually recommend charter boat companies for day sails and fishing trips

Price Categories

For a three-course
meal for one with half
a bottle of wine (or
equivalent meal), taxes,
and extra charges.

$	under $20
$$	$20–$30
$$$	$30–$45
$$$$	$45–$60
$$$$$	over $60

Off the Wall

🔟 Restaurants

1 Le St. Tropez
With an atmosphere and menu that reflect the owners' French roots, Le St. Tropez offers superb cuisine in a lovely courtyard setting. The changing menu always includes seafood items. ◈ Map A5 • 227 King St, Frederiksted • 340-772-3000 • $$$$$

2 Blue Moon
This waterfront bistro serves superb Cajun and Caribbean food (see also p31). ◈ Map A5 • 17 Strand St, Frederiksted • 340-772-2222 • $$$$

3 The Sunset Grill
This beachfront alfresco restaurant serves salads and burgers for lunch, and moves on to lobster, steak, and pasta for dinner. You can swim right off their beach. ◈ Map A5 • Rte 63, Sprat Hall, outside Frederiksted • 340-772-5855 • $$$$

4 Off the Wall
Sit at the bar or one of the in-the-sand tables at this very casual burger and sandwich spot at the water's edge. The sunsets are fabulous. ◈ Map B4 • Rte 80, Cane Bay • 340-778-4771 • $

5 Breezes
Open to the trade winds, this eatery is the place to go for Sunday brunch. After a burger, prime rib, or Caesar salad, enjoy a wedge of flourless chocolate cake dripping with fudge sauce. ◈ Map D4 • Club St. Croix, off Rte 752, Golden Rock • 340-773-7077 • $$$

6 Café Christine
French-influenced fare and divine desserts. The best seating is on the porch. ◈ Map D5 • Apothecary Hall Courtyard off Company St, Christiansted • 340-713-1500 • No dinner • $$

7 Kendrick's
Located in a picturesque old home, Kendrick's serves innovative, world-class cuisine (see also p30). Opt for the alfresco courtyard seating in good weather. ◈ Map D5 • King Cross St, Christiansted • 340-773-9199 • www.gotostcroix.com/kendricks • $$$$$

8 Restaurant Bacchus
Fine wine, befitting its name, as well as excellent food, including imaginative twists on beef, chicken, and seafood, are served at this fine restaurant (see also p30). ◈ Map D5 • Queen Cross St, Christiansted • 340-692-9922 • www.restaurantbacchus.com • $$$$

9 Rum Runners
This local favorite provides an attractive waterfront ambience and excellent food. Try the Greek salad. ◈ Map D5 • Christiansted Boardwalk at the Hotel Caravelle, Christiansted • 340-773-6585 • www.rumrunnersstcroix.com • $$$

10 Savant
Its cozy feel and a cuisine that fuses Caribbean, Mexican, and Thai has earned this restaurant a huge local following. ◈ Map D5 • Hospital St, Christiansted • 340-713-8666 • $$$$

Left **Cruz Bay** Right **Hawksnest Beach**

St. John

THE TURQUOISE WATERS, *verdant hills, and white sandy beaches of Virgin Islands National Park lure nearly one million people a year to St. John. Some spend their entire holiday at this tranquil island while others are day-trippers who come here to get away from the bustle of St. Thomas. But it's not only about peace and quiet – the small but busy towns of Cruz Bay and Coral Bay offer several good restaurants and shops. The island boasts two posh hotels and numerous condominiums, as well as two campgrounds, but many visitors opt for a more independent route and rent one of the 350 or so villas that dot the island. If you prefer a laid-back pace and don't mind that the infrastructure doesn't always work perfectly, this is the island for you.*

🔟 Sights

1. Cruz Bay
2. Hawksnest Beach
3. Jumbie Beach
4. Trunk Bay Beach
5. Cinnamon Bay Beach
6. Maho Bay Beach
7. Annaberg Plantation
8. Coral Bay
9. Bordeaux Overlook
10. Catherineberg Ruins

Popular Trunk Bay Beach

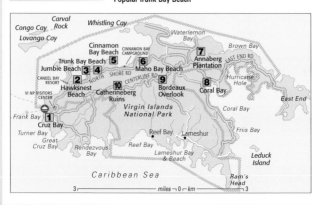

For more on Virgin Islands National Park **See pp10–11**

1 Cruz Bay

The busy ferry port at Cruz Bay is most visitors' first impression of the town and the island. But don't let the cacophony of ferry noise and taxi drivers put you off. Outside the dock, the noise abates and the town unfolds. Small, with narrow streets carrying no discernible names, Cruz Bay offers visitors the Virgin Islands National Park Visitor's Center *(see p10)*, restaurants, and shopping, but also serves as the heart of island life for St. John residents *(see pp12–13)*.

Seagrapes at Hawksnest Beach

2 Hawksnest Beach

A local favorite, Hawksnest Beach is a sandy stretch shaded by round-leafed seagrapes and towering palm trees. Keep a watch for falling coconuts. Part of the Virgin Islands National Park, the quiet beach has modest bathrooms and changing facilities, as well as shaded picnic pavilions. The snorkeling over the near-shore reefs is enjoyable, but experienced snorkelers may want to explore the rocks and pocket beach on the eastern shore. ◎ *Map D2*

3 Jumbie Beach

Another local favorite, this small, sandy beach calls for a hike down a flight of stairs. That's the easy part – you'll also have to huff and puff back up. Some trees offer shade for folk who want to go easy on their tan, and there's great snorkeling at the reef sitting just offshore. However, the water at this beach can get rough when winter swells roll in from the north. ◎ *Map D2 • Park across North Shore Rd (Rte 20)*

4 Trunk Bay Beach

Hordes of cruise ship passengers and day-trippers vie for a patch on this long, white sand beach. Palms and seagrapes provide shade, and two lifeguards ensure safety. The beach has cool showers, flush toilets, covered pavilions, a snack bar, and snorkel rentals. Its underwater snorkel trail provides an easy introduction to snorkeling and the marine world, but there is more sea life around the small island, Trunk Cay, that sits in the middle of the bay.
◎ *Map E2 • Adm (incl Annaberg Plantation) charged from 8am to 4pm*

Panoramic view of Trunk Bay

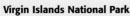

Virgin Islands National Park

Occupying a full two-thirds of the island, Virgin Islands National Park is the engine that fuels St. John. The park opened in 1956 thanks to philanthropist Laurance Rockefeller who, along with conservationist Frank Stick, had begun buying up St. John land in the 1950s. Today, the pristine and varied landscape and its historic monuments attract plenty of visitors (see pp10–11).

5 Cinnamon Bay Beach

Home to the Virgin Islands National Park campground, this beach sees lots of visitors and tour groups. But, because of its length, the groups are less of a problem here than at other beaches. For solitude, head to the far ends or come early or late. The snorkeling is particularly good at the far eastern end and around Cinnamon Cay. There are showers, flush toilets, a convenience store, and a restaurant. ◉ Map E2

6 Maho Bay Beach

While the beach at nearby Maho Bay Camps is also called Maho Bay, this stretch of greenery-fringed white sand sits adjacent to the road. There are no services, and consequently less people, which is why locals

Maho Bay Beach from North Shore Road

and boaters who moor offshore, as well as independent visitors, prefer it. The snorkeling along the beach is barely mediocre, so head to the rocks along the north edge to see colorful fish. You might see a turtle or two swim across your path. ◉ Map E2

Boiler room, Annaberg Plantation

7 Annaberg Plantation

A windmill towers over the 18th-century Annaberg Plantation, casting its long shadow on the jail cell, the old kitchen, sugar factory, the remains of the slave quarters, a garden, and other reminders of the days when slaves fueled St. John's agrarian economy. Although it can get crowded at times, most days you'll find plenty of solitude and space to enjoy the plantation's fabulous view across the sea to nearby Tortola. In summer, red flamboyant trees add splashes of color to the landscape. ◉ Map E2 • Off North Shore Rd (Rte 20) • Adm, also good at Trunk Bay Beach

8 Coral Bay

The restaurants and shops in and around Coral Bay may seem like just a stop on your round-the-island tour, but if you look a little closer you'll discover a real sense of community. Indeed, the Guy Benjamin School bears the name of a retired educator who lives just down the road. The boat yard may seem a tad on the ramshackle side, but it's the

Both Cinnamon and Maho Bay Beaches are along North Shore Rd (Rte 20)

center of life for the dozens of folks who live aboard their boats in Coral Bay harbor. ◎ *Map F2* • *East End Rd (Rte 10)*

9 Bordeaux Overlook

From this popular overlook *(see p41)*, you can admire Coral Bay below, and to the east the glorious turquoise sea, Norman Island, Peter Island, and the other islands along the BVI chain to Virgin Gorda. A tour bus favorite, the area can get quite busy with taxis and motorists trying to avoid people who wander into the road. The area also has a restaurant open for lunch and one open for dinner, plus a few gift shops. ◎ *Map E2* • *Centerline Rd (Rte 10)*

10 Catherineberg Ruins

Off the beaten path, but easy to get to, Estate Catherineberg served as headquarters for the Amina warriors during the 1733 slave uprising. The windmill and other ruins of this 1718 site are St. John's best-preserved examples of the period. To find it, turn off Centerline Road mid-island at a large Virgin Islands National Park sign. The sign is easiest to see if you're driving from Cruz Bay to Coral Bay. ◎ *Map E2* • *Centerline Rd (Rte 10)*

Catherineberg Ruins

Exploring St. John

Mid-Morning

🕐 While the air's still cool, spend an hour or two poking around snug **Cruz Bay**'s few sights and numerous shops. You can pick up a bathing suit at **Bougainvillea** *(see p68)*.

Take time to sit awhile on **Cruz Bay Park**'s benches. The shady park with its flower-fringed walkways serves as the town's crossroads *(see p13)*.

After shopping and people-watching take a break for lunch at the popular **Lime Inn** *(see p69)*.

Afternoon

Gorgeous white sandy beaches fringe the coast. Pick the one that most appeals to you. If you'd like some quiet, **Maho Bay Beach** may be your best option. Just park along the road and stretch out on the beach for an hour or two in the sun or, more wisely, in the shade of the seagrape trees.

After a swim and a snorkel, make the brief drive along the North Shore Road to the **Annaberg Plantation** cut-off. A visit to the sugar plantation ruins will take about 20 minutes, unless you spend time absorbing the spectacular view of the sea and nearby Tortola or walking along the shore.

Late Afternoon

Continue along North Shore Road until you meet Centerline Road. Make a quick trip to **Coral Bay** for late afternoon drinks and a chance to mingle with the local folks at **Skinny Legs Bar & Restaurant** *(see p69)* before heading back to Cruz Bay.

For more on the 1733 Slave Rebellion **See p48**

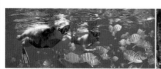 

Left **Snorkeling** Right **Hikers, Reef Bay Hike**

Outdoor Activities

1 Day Sails
Book a day sail to an offshore cay at your hotel or through Connections or Adventures in Paradise in Cruz Bay. ✆ *Connections; Map D2; 3340-776-6922 • Adventures in Paradise; Map D2; 3340-779-4527*

2 Fishing
Charter boats leave from the Cruz Bay waterfront on fishing trips to North or South Drops. Captain Byron Oliver also offers trips closer to St. John. ✆ *Capt. Oliver • 340-693-8339*

3 Hiking
There are hiking trails all over the island. Some are easy treks over flat terrain, but others can test your endurance as you head up, up, uphill. ✆ *VINP Visitor's Center • Map D2 • 340-776-6201*

4 Horseback Riding
Clip-clop along quiet lanes and pebbly beaches with Carolina Corral, located just outside Coral Bay. Trips lasting one hour leave from Route 107 across from the restaurant Time for a Break. ✆ *Map F2 • 340-693-5778*

5 Kayaking
Rent a kayak from hotels. Arawak Expeditions at Low Key Watersports in Cruz Bay does day trips and overnight sojourns. ✆ *Map D2 • 340-693-8312*

6 Scuba
Several watersports centers run dive trips to offshore and in-shore reefs, and to the Wreck of the Rhone in the BVI. ✆ *Low Key Watersports, Wharfside Village, Cruz Bay; Map D2; 340-693-8999 • Cruz Bay Watersports, Boulon Center Rd, Cruz Bay; Map D2; 340-776-6234 & Westin Resort, Great Cruz Bay; Map D2; 340-693-8000*

7 Snorkeling
Just stroll off the beach and head for the rocks or the reefs to see colorful fish and sea life. Practice first in knee-high water to get the hang of it.

8 Swimming
Clear, warm water with high salt content makes it easy to float. Join the locals for their early morning or late afternoon swims along the island's beaches.

Windsurfing, Cinnamon Bay

9 Tennis
The Westin Resort *(see p115)* lets in non-guests to its six lighted courts for a small fee. Or play with the locals on the public tennis courts near the fire station in Cruz Bay.

10 Windsurfing
Rent sailboards at breezy Cinnamon Bay Beach *(see p64)* for an exhilarating trip around the bay. The staff give lessons for novices or for those who want to improve their skills.

Left **Caneel Hill** Center **Ram's Head** Right **Sign of the Cinnamon Bay Ruins Trail**

TOP 10 Short Hikes

1 Caneel Hill Trail
This 2-mile (3-km) trail leaves from near Mongoose Junction Shopping Center (see p68) in Cruz Bay, goes past a scenic overlook, and connects with the North Shore Road near Caneel Bay Resort (see p112).

2 Peace Hill
An enchanting spot with fine views in three directions reached by a short walk uphill, this is just right for a picnic. ◈ North Shore Rd

3 Cinnamon Bay Long Trail
Running downhill from Centerline Road to North Shore Road near Cinnamon Bay Campground (see p115), this 1.1-mile (1.7-km) trail offers superb views.

4 Cinnamon Bay Ruins Trail
Signs describing the flora, fauna, and historical features mark this half-mile (1-km) loop trail. It starts and ends at the sugar factory ruins near Cinnamon Bay Campground. ◈ North Shore Rd

5 Francis Bay Trail
With mangroves and salt ponds along the way, the half-mile (1-km) long Francis Bay Trail is a bird-watcher's favorite. ◈ Off North Shore Rd

6 Brown Bay Trail
Hike about a mile (1.6 km) from Waterlemon Bay along the Johnny Horn Trail to reach the Brown Bay Trail, which leads to the bay and its remote snorkeling.

7 Ram's Head Trail
Walk 1 mile (1.6 km) uphill from Salt Pond Bay across a rocky beach and hills of cacti to a spectacular view. A local favorite on full-moon nights. ◈ Rte 107

8 Lameshur
This area has three trails. The short Yawzi Point Trail leads from the beach to a promontory. The Lameshur and Bordeaux trails start just past the beach at the road's end; the first is 1 mile (1.6 km) to Reef Bay and the second runs about a mile uphill to Bordeaux Road. ◈ Off Rte 107

9 Reef Bay Trail
While you can trek the 2.2 miles (3.5 km) from Centerline Road to the ruins at the Reef Bay Plantation by yourself, a Virgin Islands National Park trip provides a boat ride back to Cruz Bay (see also p11). ◈ 340-776-6201

10 Petroglyphs
A short trail heads off the Reef Bay Trail to pools rimed with petroglyphs, possibly inscribed by Taino Indians.

Left **Bougainvillea Boutique** Center **Caravan Gallery** Right **Pink Papaya**

🔟 Shopping

1 Bamboula
Trendy tropical clothes, housewares with style, and plenty of knick-knacks crowd the shelves of this spacious store. 🌐 *Map D2 • Mongoose Junction Shopping Center • 340-693-8699*

2 Bougainvillea Boutique
Look for very chic tropical wear, including bathing suits that make less-than-perfect figures look great, and flattering hats at this pricey boutique. 🌐 *Map D2 • Mongoose Junction Shopping Center • 340-693-7190*

3 Caravan Gallery
Shop here for unusual jewelry at reasonable prices. Special items, such as the sea life globes with falling glitter, make fun gifts. 🌐 *Map D2 • Mongoose Junction Shopping Center • 340-779-4566*

Jewelry at R&I Patton

4 Fabric Mill
Bolts of colorful fabric, table linen with tropical allure, batik wraps to use on the beach, and soft toys with marine motifs fill this store. 🌐 *Map D2 • Mongoose Junction Shopping Center • 340-776-6194*

5 R&I Patton
While this store carries all sorts of jewelry, it stakes its reputation on gold and silver pieces crafted in tropical motifs. Look for hibiscus, sugar mills, and more. 🌐 *Map D2 • Mongoose Junction Shopping Center • 340-776-6548*

6 Wicker, Wood & Shells
With an upstairs art gallery carrying the best from local and international artists, this store also has a downstairs gift shop. It's the place to go for Christmas ornaments. 🌐 *Map D2 • Mongoose Junction Shopping Center • 340-776-6909*

7 St. John Editions
Nifty cotton dresses that do double duty as beach cover-ups, straw hats, colorful bags, casual jewelry, and accessories from this shop round off your tropical wardrobe. 🌐 *Map D2 • North Shore Rd (Rte 20), Cruz Bay • 340-693-8444*

8 Pink Papaya
Gift items ranging from coloring books to tea pots and dinnerware sets splashed in bright colors. 🌐 *Map D2 • Lemon Tree Mall, King St, Cruz Bay • 340-693-8535*

9 Mumbo Jumbo
This pleasant store offers clothes, canvas bags, toys, and gift items galore at what may be the best prices in St. John. 🌐 *Map F2 • Skinny Legs Shopping Complex, East End Rd (Rte 10) • 340-779-4277*

10 Jolly Dog
In addition to Jolly Dog logo t-shirts and hats, this tiny store stocks bright beach towels, sarongs, and souvenirs such as mugs and locally made hot sauce. 🌐 *Map F2 • Shipwreck Landing, Rte 107, Sanders Bay • 340-693-5333*

Price Categories

For a three-course meal for one with half a bottle of wine (or equivalent meal), taxes, and extra charges.

$	under $20
$$	$20–$30
$$$	$30–$45
$$$$	$45–$60
$$$$$	over $60

Skinny Legs Bar & Restaurant

🔟 Restaurants

1 Fish Trap
Early-bird specials and a menu that includes pasta, fish, and conch fritters at this casual place. ✪ Bay & Strand Sts, next to Our Lady of Mount Carmel Church, Cruz Bay • 340-693-9994 • No lunch • $$$

2 Lime Inn
This local favorite offers lots of fish, chicken, beef, and pasta dishes. The Wednesday night all-you-can-eat of its spicy shrimp brings out diners in droves. ✪ Lemon Tree Mall, King St, Cruz Bay • 340-776-6425 • No lunch Sat • $$$$

3 Panini Beach
Opt for the terrace tables at this beachfront bistro in good weather. Delicious pizzas and pastas (see p31). ✪ Wharfside Village, Cruz Bay • 340-693-9119 • $$$$

4 Chloe & Bernard's
Sample international cuisine at this airy restaurant at the Westin Resort (see p115). ✪ South Shore Rd (Rte 104), Great Cruz Bay • 340-693-8000 • No lunch • $$$$$

5 Zozo's Ristorante
Imaginative food is coupled with lovely presentation. ✪ Gallows Point Resort, Bay St, Cruz Bay • 340-693-9200 • No lunch • $$$$$

6 Asolare
Its Asian-inspired changing menu and sunset views set the stage for a lovely dinner. Don't miss the chocolate pyramid cake (see p30). ✪ North Shore Rd (Rte 20), Caneel Hill outside Cruz Bay • 340-779-4747 • No lunch • $$$$$

7 Chateaux Bordeaux
One of the island's finest, with an inspired international menu and a good wine list (see p30). ✪ Centerline Rd (Rte 10), Bordeaux • 340-776-6611 • No lunch • $$$$$

8 Skinny Legs Bar & Restaurant
Slightly ramshackle but hugely popular, this yachtie spot dishes up the best burgers, beers, and big screen television sports (see p31). ✪ East End Rd (Rte 10), Coral Bay • 340-779-4982 • $

9 Vie's Snack Shack
Stop by Vie's frontyard for conch fritters, fried chicken, and tarts. ✪ East End Rd (Rte 10), Hansen Bay • 340-693-5033 • No dinner • $

10 Miss Lucy's
This seaside place serves its Caribbean food with style. Tasty paella created from local seafood. ✪ Rte 107, Friis Bay • 340-693-5244 • $$$

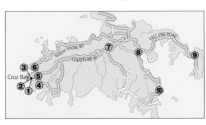

Following pages **Sign of Off the Wall restaurant, St. Croix**

Left **Charlotte Amalie harbor** Right **Havensight Mall**

St. Thomas

WITH LUSH HILLSIDES, white beaches, and boat-filled harbors, St. Thomas packs a lot into its 28 sq miles (72 sq km). Visitors can opt to stay at a casual, in-town guesthouse, a home-like condominium, or a posh beachfront resort. Restaurants run from bare bones to many stars. Fine beaches, excellent duty-free shopping, the exciting Coral World marine park (see pp18–19), and plenty of watersports beckon travelers, while there is easy transportation to Virgin Islands National Park in St. John, nearby Tortola in the BVI, and, a bit farther afield, St. Croix. This pint-sized patch in the Caribbean can be most things to many people – spend one day at the beach, the next touring historic sites, the day after on a day sail, scuba dive, or sightseeing on a sister island. Or you may choose to do nothing at all.

10 Sights

1. Charlotte Amalie
2. Havensight
3. Frenchtown
4. Crown Bay
5. University of the Virgin Islands
6. Drake's Seat
7. Magens Bay Beach
8. Tillett Gardens/ Tutu
9. Compass Point
10. Red Hook

Magens Bay Beach

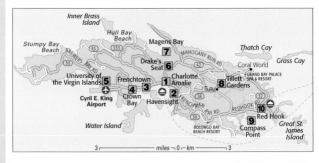

1 Charlotte Amalie

This bustling town hides its history behind the doors of busy shops, but savvy strollers stop for a look at the buildings' interesting architecture and old stone walls. The town area

Inside a bar in Frenchtown

is anchored by the huge red Fort Christian on the east and, to the west, the covered market where planters once bought slaves, now used as a produce and crafts market. To the south sits a lively harbor, and, to the north, hillside streets filled with colonial homes and other historic buildings *(see pp16–17)*.

2 Havensight

Home to the island's largest cruise ship pier, the thriving Havensight area has a major shopping mall as its heart *(see p14)*. Catering mainly to cruise ship passengers, the mall also attracts shoppers who don't want to head to the downtown Charlotte Amalie shopping area. Tourist shops selling jewelry, electronics, and gift items sit alongside a bank, the island's only real bookstore, and a handful of restaurants. More shops, a grocery store, and several restaurants line Havensight Road.
Ⓢ *Map B2 • Havensight Rd (Rte 30)*

Cruise Capital

St. Thomas may just be the cruise ship capital of the Caribbean. On busy winter days, as many as eight or occasionally more cruise ships visit Charlotte Amalie. Most go to Havensight dock, while a few tie up at Crown Bay. Thousands of passengers go shopping, enjoy watersports, take tours, and just about stretch the island's tourism infrastructure to the limit.

3 Frenchtown

Located on the peninsula to the west of Charlotte Amalie, Frenchtown was settled several centuries ago by a tiny community of people from the French island of St. Barthélemy. Most Frenchtown residents earn their living from the sea. They sell their fish along the harbor front or to any of the many eateries that make Frenchtown so popular. Some of the island's best restaurants are found in this small, relatively quiet neighborhood, so it's worth your while to stroll the narrow lanes looking for an appealing dinner or lunch spot. If you're in Frenchtown around July 14, attend the Bastille Day celebrations – these are held every year at the ballfield. Ⓢ *Map B2 • Off Veterans Dr (Rte 30)*

4 Crown Bay

Only a few cruise ships tie up at the Crown Bay dock; most go to Havensight. Facilities are minimal around the pier, so you'll have to walk a few blocks to the Crown Bay Marina and shopping complex to find restaurants and a gourmet grocery. A few more restaurants and a couple of shops flank the busy road that runs from the pier to the Crown Bay Marina. If you are there in winter, visit the marina for a gander at the multimillion-dollar yachts that stop by St. Thomas.
Ⓢ *Map B2 • Off Moravian Hwy (Rte 30)*

Left **University of the Virgin Islands** Right **Tillett Gardens**

5 University of the Virgin Islands

This seaside university offers associate, bachelor's, and graduate degrees to students from all over the Caribbean on a prestigious campus that served the US military during World War II. The school held its first classes in 1963 as a junior college. Attend performances that range from ballet to reggae at the school's Reichhold Center for the Arts (see p45), see games at the UVI Sports and Fitness Complex, take a swim at the white, sandy Brewers Bay Beach, or just stroll the spacious grounds. ◎ Map B2 • Brewers Bay Rd (Rte 30) • www.uvi.edu

6 Drake's Seat

Legend has it that the 16th-century explorer Sir Francis Drake kept tabs on his troops

View from Drake's Seat

from this spot (see p41). Today, it's often busy with taxi drivers stopping to let passengers enjoy the stupendous view of Magens Bay, St. John, and the entire BVI chain to the east. A small parking lot sits on the north side of the narrow road, with the seat – not the original – just across the road. There can be a lot of traffic, so be careful crossing the street. ◎ Map B2 • Rte 40

7 Magens Bay Beach

The most beautiful beach in St. Thomas, the long and spacious Magens Bay Beach is usually full of people. It's the number one spot visitors want to see. The beach has a restaurant, watersports rentals, a nature trail, bathrooms, showers, and on weekends, crowds of locals who come to party to amplified music. While all this activity may not be your cup of tea, if you find yourself there, just head to the far ends of the beach for some quiet. ◎ Map B2 • Rte 35

8 Tillett Gardens/Tutu

An oasis of quiet in the busiest area in St. Thomas, Tillett Gardens is a courtyard filled with a handful of arty shops definitely worth a look. Back into the traffic and congestion that hallmarks the rest of the area, there are several large shopping malls with grocery stores, one of the island's two Kmart department stores (see p14), and other chain shops. This area is also the heart of fast food eating in St. Thomas. The enclosed Tutu Park Mall has a small food court and public bathrooms. ✆ Map C2 • Smith Bay Rd (Rte 38)

9 Compass Point

The village of Compass Point is home to a small collection of shops and restaurants, which serve the dozens of old salts who live aboard or keep their boats at the marina as well as any visitors who happen to wander by. Park your car in the lot to the left as you reach the area. Rent watersports equipment down on the dock or people-watch as you enjoy your lunch at the snack wagon or dinner at one of the restaurants. ✆ Map C2 • Off Red Hook Rd (Rte 32)

Ferry dock at Red Hook

10 Red Hook

Busy Red Hook serves as the jumping-off spot for trips to St. John. The ferry dock hums with activity until midnight, when the ferries stop running. The strip of highway that runs through its several blocks is flanked with stores selling just about anything you'd need on an island vacation. You'll find a grocery store, a pharmacy, a gas station, a place to get your photos developed, a handful of restaurants ranging from take-out Chinese to seafood, and a gift shop or two. ✆ Map C2 • Red Hook Rd (Rte 32)

A Leisurely Drive

Mid-Morning

Located at the eastern end, **Red Hook** makes the perfect starting point for your island tour. Pick your stops so you'll have time and energy to enjoy the island's main attraction – the beach. Follow Red Hook Road, perhaps pausing for a stroll around **Compass Point**, before heading to the busy **Tillett Gardens/Tutu** area. To watch artisans at work, pull into Tillett Gardens. Or stop at Tutu Park Mall for anything you need.

Shop for take-home gifts at the malls at **Havensight**, or wait until you reach **Charlotte Amalie**.

Once there, spend a little time poking around the shops housed in old warehouses and the historic sites before breaking for Caribbean-inspired French fare at **Hervé Restaurant** (see p79), located a flight of stairs uphill on Government Hill.

Afternoon

Keep along Veterans Drive, making side trips at **Frenchtown** for the seafaring ambience and at **Crown Bay** for the megayachts. Veterans Drive turns into Brewers Bay Road and takes you past the **University of the Virgin Islands** campus. Continue along the island's spine till you see the splendid views at **Drake's Seat**.

Late Afternoon

End your day with a swim at **Magens Bay Beach**. The crowds are gone, the beach is quiet unless it's the weekend, and the residents come out to enjoy the serenity.

Left **Atlantis Adventures sign** Center **Seaplane at Charlotte Amalie** Right **Mountain Top bar**

10 Things to Do

1 Coral World

Get a taste of the marine life that surrounds St. Thomas without the need to get wet, although that is an option with some of the activities *(see pp18–19)*.

2 Atlantis Adventures

Look out for darting fish and colorful reefs from the portholes of the submarine *(see p39)*. The captain and crew narrate the trip. ◎ *Map B2 • Havensight Mall, Havensight Rd (Rte 30) • 340-776-5650*

3 St. Thomas Skyride

Ride the cable car for great views from 700 ft (210 m) above the harbor. ◎ *Map B2 • Long Bay Rd (Rte 30), Havensight • 340-774-9809 • www.stthomasskyride.com*

4 Estate St. Peter Mountain Great House

This estate overlooking Magens Bay includes a spacious great house and botanical garden with varieties of plants, waterfalls, fish ponds, and a bird sanctuary. ◎ *Map B2 • St. Peter Mountain Rd (Rte 40) • 340-774-1724 • www.greathouse-mountaintop.com*

5 Mountain Top

This restaurant and shopping complex offers superb views of the island chain. The bar's banana daiquiris are famous. ◎ *Map B2 • Off St. Peter Mountain Rd (Rte 40)*

6 Round-the-island Tour

This is the best way to see the sights of St. Thomas if you're here for only a day. The Havensight cruise ship pier is a convenient place to catch a cab.

7 Helicopter Tour

Get a bird's-eye view of the turquoise waters, white sand beaches, and charming towns in St. Thomas and St. John. Longer trips include the BVI. ◎ *Leaves from north side of Cyril E. King Airport • Brewers Bay Rd (Rte 30) • Map B2 • 340-775-7335 • www.aircenterhelicopters.com*

8 Day Trip to St. Croix

A 25-minute seaplane flight from the Charlotte Amalie waterfront to Christiansted, St. Croix, lets you explore the slower pace of this historic town. ◎ *Seaborne Airlines; Map B2; 888-359-8687; www.seaborneairlines.com • Cape Air; Map B2; 800-352-0714; www.capeair.com*

9 Day Trip to St. John

Hop the ferry at Red Hook or Charlotte Amalie to Cruz Bay and spend a day exploring Virgin Islands National Park. ◎ *20 mins from Red Hook ferry dock; Map C2 • 45 mins from Charlotte Amalie; Map B2*

10 Day Trip to Tortola

Ferries run from Red Hook and the Edward Wilmoth Blyden ferry terminal in Charlotte Amalie to Road Town or West End in Tortola, which are very different from the USVI towns. ◎ *From Red Hook, Map C2, 1 hr to West End & Road Town • From Charlotte Amalie, Map B2, 1/2 hr to West End & 1 hr 15 mins to Road Town*

Red Hook ferry dock is on Red Hook Rd (Rte 32) and the Charlotte Amalie waterfront terminal on Veterans Dr (Rte 30)

Left **Sport fishing boats at a St. Thomas marina** Right **Mahogany Run Golf Course**

🔟 Outdoor Activities

1 Day Sails
Go sailing for a day of sun and snorkeling aboard one of the many charter boats that head to St. John or an offshore cay.

2 Fishing
Charters depart from marinas at the island's east end for the North Drop, located off St. Thomas and St. John and home to wahoo, bonito, kingfish, black-fin or yellowfin tuna, and marlin.

3 Golf
Play the famed Devil's Triangle at the 18-hole Mahogany Run Golf Course. It overlooks the ocean, adding great views to your golf game. ◈ Map C2 • Mahogany Run Rd (Rte 42) • 340-777-6006 • www.mahoganyrungolf.com

4 Kayaking
Rent kayaks at oceanfront hotels for a paddle around the bay or take a kayaking and snorkel tour through a mangrove-fringed lagoon with Virgin Islands Ecotours. ◈ Map C2 • Virgin Islands Ecotours, Nadir Rd (Rte 32) • 340-779-2155 • www.viecotours.com

5 Parasailing
Many companies take you about 400 ft (120 m) over the Caribbean Sea in a parasail. Most hotels and villas can help with arrangements for pick-ups at a waterfront hotel.

6 Personal Watercraft
Zip around the harbor and beyond on a wave runner, but be careful around the boats. You can rent watercraft from Bolongo Bay Beach Club (see p115) and Sapphire Beach Resort (see p117).

7 Scuba
Major hotels, beaches, and marinas have dive centers. You can also take a boat trip to scuba-dive around the reefs and wrecks that sit off St. Thomas (see p25).

8 Snorkeling
There's nothing simpler than snorkeling. Put on a mask, snorkel, and fins, plop into the water, and away you go over reefs and fish.

9 Tennis
All major hotels and many smaller ones have lighted tennis courts open to non-guests for a fee. Another option is to play with the locals at the two lighted public courts at Subbase. ◈ Map B2 • Off Moravian Hwy (Rte 30)

Parasailing in St. Thomas

🔟 Windsurfing
Most beachfront hotels rent wind-surfers. Or try the granddaddy of wind-surfing operations in St. Thomas, West Indies Windsurfing. ◈ Map C2 • West Indies Windsurfing, Vessup Beach, Nazareth • 340-775-6530

West Indies Windsurfing gives lessons in windsurfing and rents equipment

Left **Crystal, A.H. Riise** Center **Chocolates** Right **Color of Joy**

🔟 Shops

1 A.H. Riise
Housed in an historic sugar warehouse, this large department store *(see p15)* is filled with crystal, jewelry, art, and an array of gift items. ✎ *Map N2 • 37 Main St, Charlotte Amalie*

2 Cardow Jewelers
This venerable jewelry store has fine pieces in all price ranges. ✎ *Map P2 • 39 Main St, Charlotte Amalie*

3 Tropicana Perfume Shop
Luscious scents from top brands such as Guerlain, Chanel, Lancôme, Estée Lauder, Dior, Borghese, and Sisley waft out to greet you at this perfumery. ✎ *Map P2 • 2 Main St, Charlotte Amalie*

4 Little Switzerland
The trademark red shopping bags of this brand go home filled with stunning, pricey crystal, china, jewelry, and gifts. ✎ *Map N3; Main St & Map P3; Tolbod Gade, Charlotte Amalie • Map B2; Havensight Mall*

5 Royal Caribbean
Known for its cameras and accessories, this store also sells jewelry, watches and other

Tropicana Perfume Shop

electronics. ✎ *Map N2; Main St, Charlotte Amalie • Map B2; Havensight Mall*

6 Caribbean Chocolate
Step in for Godiva chocolates and other tempting treats. Candy melts fast in the tropics – make this your last stop. ✎ *Map N3 • 1 Trompeter Gade, Charlotte Amalie*

7 Cosmopolitan
This store carries the most elegant wear for men and women from top designers. Look for brands such as Cosci, Gottex, Bruno Magli, A. Testoni, Fratelli, and Paul & Shark. ✎ *Map N3 • Veterans Dr (Rte 30), Charlotte Amalie*

8 Down Island Traders
Rum cakes, jams, spices, and seasoning from this store make inexpensive gifts. You can also get canvas bags and more, with tropical motifs. ✎ *Map P3 • Veterans Dr (Rte 30), Charlotte Amalie*

9 Tradewinds Shop
You'll get distinctive gift items here, such as nifty metal sea sculptures, decorative tiles, and fish carved from coral, plus Naot sandals, best for tropical trekking. ✎ *Map N3 • Veterans Dr (Rte 30), Charlotte Amalie*

10 Color of Joy
Artist Corrine Van Rensselaer showcases her own and the work of other island artists, as well as tropical gift items, at her small gallery. ✎ *Map C2 • Rte 322 near Ritz-Carlton Hotel*

Agave Terrace

Price Categories	
For a three-course meal for one with half a bottle of wine (or equivalent meal), taxes, and extra charges.	**$** under $20
	$$ $20–$30
	$$$ $30–$45
	$$$$ $45–$60
	$$$$$ over $60

Restaurants

1 Craig & Sally's
The ambience at this cozy place centers around wine, with an ever-changing menu. ◈ Off Veterans Dr (Rte 30), Frenchtown • 340-777-9949 • No lunch Sat–Tue • $$$$$

2 Epernay
The sophisticated fare here runs to sushi. Transforms into a swinging night club on some days (see p37). ◈ Off Veterans Dr (Rte 30), Frenchtown • 340-774-5348 • $$$

3 Hook, Line & Sinker
The setting is pedestrian, but the food is something to write home about. Try the delicious homemade chicken noodle soup. ◈ Off Veterans Dr (Rte 30), Frenchtown • 340-776-9708 • $$$

4 Hervé Restaurant
Caribbean-flavored French food (see p30). ◈ Government Hill, Charlotte Amalie • 340-777-9703 • $$$$

5 Texas Pit Barbecue
The best barbecued chicken, ribs, and brisket dished up from trucks across St. Thomas. ◈ Red Hook Rd (Rte 32) across from the ferry dock • Wheatley Center (Raphune Hill) • Charlotte Amalie waterfront • Veterans Dr (Rte 30) • Subbase (Off Rte 30) • $

6 Virgilio's Restaurant
Air-conditioned Virgilio's creates North Italian fare with subtle

seasonings (see p30). ◈ Off Main St on Store Tvaer Gade, Charlotte Amalie • 340-693-0428 • $$$$$

7 Randy's Bistro
Unassuming Randy's is a local favorite. The menu features imaginative takes on seafood, chicken, and beef entrées. ◈ Al Cohen Mall, Weymouth Rhymer Hwy (Rte 38) • 340-777-3199 • $$$$

8 Romano's Restaurant
North Italian fare at its finest. The pan seared salmon Veronique is superb (see p31). ◈ Off Smith Bay Rd (Rte 38), Smith Bay • 340-775-0045 • No lunch • $$$$$

9 Agave Terrace
While seafood stars here, the menu sports choices such as tenderloin steak for carnivores (see p31). ◈ Point Pleasant Resort, Smith Bay Rd (Rte 38), Smith Bay • 340-775-4142 • No lunch • $$$$$

10 Blue Moon Café
Try the red snapper with pecans, bananas, and coconut rum sauce here (see p31). ◈ Secret Harbour Beach Resort, off Rte 322 • 340-779-2262 • $$$$

Left **Village Marina Cay** Right **Apple Bay**

Tortola

THE ISLAND OF TORTOLA BLENDS BUSTLE *with bucolic. Its main town, Road Town, is the center of an off-shore banking industry, a port for cruise ships plying the Caribbean, and the jumping-off spot for trips to other BVI islands. It can get busy when office workers and tourists fill its lanes and shopping centers. However, the peace of rural Tortola is just moments away. The stunning palm-fringed beaches are rarely crowded, and only a couple of cars can be spotted moving along the narrow roads that crisscross the island's green hills. Enjoy the intimacy of its small hotels and the thrill of the vast array of watersports on offer. Indeed, the entire BVI is a major sailing capital of the world and many week-long charters depart from Tortola's many marinas.*

10 Sights

1. Road Town
2. Fort Burt
3. Nanny Cay
4. West End
5. Smuggler's Cove
6. Apple Bay
7. Cane Garden Bay
8. Brewers Bay
9. Lambert Beach
10. Beef Island

Road Town

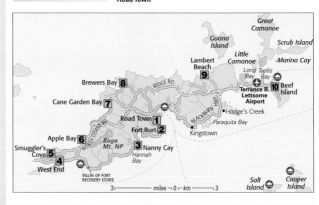

1 Road Town

The heart of the island's commerce and tourism industry, harborfront Road Town buzzes with cruise ship tourists and office workers crowding its streets for lunch or to shop. Its narrow Main Street is lined with small old wooden and stone buildings. Road Town spills out to the east with Wickhams Cay I, home to a couple of hotels, and numerous shops, restaurants, and offices, just a short walk from Main Street. Charter yachts pick up or drop off passengers here and at Wickhams Cay II, a mile (1.6 km) away along Waterfront Drive. ◎ Map H4

Road sign, West End

2 Fort Burt

Now hidden behind a hotel façade, Fort Burt was built in the 17th century by the Dutch to protect Road Town. In 1776, the English rebuilt the fort and named it after William Burt, who then served as governor for the chain of Caribbean Islands known as the Leeward. In 1953, the fort was turned into a hotel. It's worth wandering in to see the thick walls and ramparts, stopping for a drink at the hotel bar. Parking is difficult – it's easiest to leave your car at the bottom of the hill and walk up. ◎ Map H4 • Waterfront Dr

3 Nanny Cay

While all things nautical are the focus at Nanny Cay and its marina, it also makes a pleasant stop for folks taking in the sights. It has a few restaurants and interesting shops. Wander the adjacent boat yard to watch boat owners and crews at work maintaining their spiffy yachts. To try out the lifestyle, book a charter at the hotel or rent a power boat for a day on the blue Caribbean waters. ◎ Map H5 • Waterfront Dr

4 West End

This area gets busy when the ferries from St. Thomas, St. John, and Jost Van Dyke arrive. If you're arriving from outside the BVI, you'll clear BVI Customs and Immigration here. The area around the ferry dock has a couple of basic restaurants and convenience stores. Soper's Hole marina with restaurants and shops sits within walking distance across the harbor. There are small hotels near the ferry dock and the marina. ◎ Map G5 • Waterfront Dr

5 Smuggler's Cove

Put your Jeep in four-wheel drive for a ride down a rutted dirt road to this gorgeous beach. Just keep going past Long Bay Beach Resort (see p117) on the North Coast Road. Taxi drivers will drop you off with a promise to pick you up at the appointed hour. While it's a bit of an adventure getting there, the pristine beach and great snorkeling await you. Bring a picnic lunch. ◎ Map G5
• Off North Coast Rd

Smuggler's Cove

Left **Cane Garden Bay** Right **Brewers Bay**

6 Apple Bay

The waves sometimes roll at Apple Bay, particularly during the winter season, making this one of the better surfing spots in the Virgin Islands. When it's calm, the water is fine for swimming. Nearly a mile (1.6 km) in length with white sand as well as some rocks, Apple Bay Beach never gets crowded, so pull over and pick your spot. There are a couple of small but distinctive lodging and restaurant options located at either end of the beach, with the absolutely outrageous Bomba Shack bar *(see p37)* near the western end. ⊗ *Map G4 • North Coast Rd*

Bomba Shack bar, Apple Bay

Brits Rule – Maybe

A good-sized British expatriate population calls Tortola home, lured by the tropical climate and the British flag flying overhead. While the schools and courts use the British system and you can buy British biscuits in the supermarkets, the influence stops there. The island has a decidedly American feel and American dollars are the legal tender, both thanks to the nearby US Virgin Islands.

7 Cane Garden Bay

The North Coast Road runs right through Cane Garden Bay, a small community that's home to a handful of guesthouses, and a few casual West Indian restaurants that can really get hopping when music plays. Make a stop at the venerable Callwood Rum Distillery *(see p21)*, where the Callwood family has brewed rum for decades. Boaters like to anchor offshore for a stretch on the long sandy beach and, of course, to enjoy the restaurants and nightlife together with hotel guests. ⊗ *Map G4 • North Coast Rd*

8 Brewers Bay

Make sure your brakes work before you drive way downhill to Brewers Bay. Both Brewers Bay East and Brewers Bay West Roads, leading to the bay, are super steep. The beach itself is a long stretch of sand with calm water that sees few people other than those visiting Brewers Bay Campground. This collection of tents and shelters nestles at the water's edge. The campground's small restaurant serves modest meals; but it's best to bring lunch and snacks because the eatery keeps irregular hours. Excellent swimming and snorkeling are enough reasons to make the trip. ✎ Map H4 • Brewers Bay W Rd

9 Lambert Beach

Sometimes called Elizabeth Beach, this is a fine strand of palm- and seagrape-fringed sand where you may see a nesting leatherback turtle crawl up during the spring and early summer months. Take Ridge Road to Lambert Road, then turn left at the sign for Lambert Estates through an area of scattered upscale homes and a small resort. Stop for lunch at the alfresco Turtle Restaurant, located at Lambert Beach Resort. ✎ Map J4 • Lambert Rd

10 Beef Island

This small island is home to the BVI's largest airport, officially called Terrance B. Lettsome International Airport (see p96) after a former member of the BVI Legislative Council. Pay your 50-cent toll to cross the Beef Island Bridge by putting the money in a cup extended by the toll collector. Beef Island's long, lovely beach draws numerous swimmers and shellers. Its Trellis Bay is also the jumping off point for ferry trips to smaller islands, and has a small collection of shops and restaurants. ✎ Map J4

Beef Island Bridge

A Walk in Road Town

Mid-Morning

🕐 Center your stroll on Road Town, leaving busy places such as Wickhams Cay I to the office workers and frenetic shoppers. Start at the Post Office, where philatelists can buy the island's spectacular stamps. Meander up narrow Main Street, poking in and out of small shops selling essentials as well as knick-knacks. Main Street just about ends at **Sunny Caribbee** (see p43), where you can browse for Caribbean spices and jams and enjoy the colorful artwork at its sister gallery.

Cross the Waterfront Highway for a stroll through **Crafts Alive**, one of the best spots to shop for locally made crafts (see p43). The artisans are often on hand to discuss their wares.

Stop by the waterfront ferry terminal to watch islanders coming and going. Boats leave for the USVI and outer BVIs throughout the day, so you'll get an eye-opening view into island life as you watch folks lug groceries, huge boxes, and all manner of things onto the ferries. The air-conditioned waiting room provides a chilly respite if the warm weather has you dripping. Pick up a copy of the tourist publication, The BVI Welcome (see p100), for a good read while you rest.

Having no doubt worked up an appetite, amble along Waterfront Drive for cold drinks and delicious Italian fare at **Capriccio di Mare** (see p85), a hot spot for locals on their lunch break.

Left **Ferry from Road Town to Virgin Gorda** Right **Sage Mountain National Park**

TOP 10 Outdoor Activities

1 Day Sails
Crewed boats leave from Road Town, Nanny Cay, and Soper's Hole for an offshore cay, Jost Van Dyke, the Baths on Virgin Gorda, or Anegada.

2 Fishing
Fish in the North Drop and other locations. For bonefishing, Caribbean Fly Fishing is the best.
⊗ Caribbean Fly Fishing • 284-494-4797
• www.caribflyfishing.com

3 Hiking
Sage Mountain National Park (see p20) is crisscrossed with shady hiking trails, none of them particularly strenuous or busy. Spend hours enjoying the solitude. ⊗ Map G5
• 284-494-3904 (for hiking inquiries)

Kayaking

4 Horseback Riding
Shadow Stables takes you trotting along beautiful, deserted beaches and up and down Tortola's hills. The island takes on a new perspective when viewed from the saddle, and spectacular vistas are all around. ⊗ Map H4
• Ridge Rd, Todman Peak • 284-494-2262

5 Kayaking
Many resorts offer complimentary kayak use for a paddle around their bay. Otherwise, you can rent them at Nanny Cay, Trellis Bay, or Cane Garden Bay for a paddling and snorkeling excursion.

6 Scuba
Many week-long or more sailing charters specialize in scuba-diving the wrecks that sit offshore. Or sign on with any of the marina-based dive operators for a day trip.

7 Snorkeling
If you don't have your own gear, you can easily rent mask, snorkel, and fins from watersports centers all over the island. Look for dark patches near the shore that indicate rocks, reefs, or seagrass beds.

8 Swimming
Enjoy great swimming off the BVI – dive in from your charter boat or do laps off the beach for some easy and efficient exercise, or just float in the waters and enjoy the landscape.

9 Tennis
Frenchman's Cay Hotel (see p113), Long Bay Beach Resort (see p117), and Prospect Reef Resort (see p116) let non-guests play their courts for a fee. Play free at Moorings-Mariner Inn (see p116) if the court is not in use.

10 Windsurfing
Brisk trade winds, particularly at Trellis Bay, lure windsurfers to Tortola. Rent boards at Trellis Bay and Nanny Cay. You can also take lessons. ⊗ Map J4, H5

Price Categories

For a three-course
meal for one with half
a bottle of wine (or
equivalent meal), taxes,
and extra charges.

$	under $20
$$	$20–$30
$$$	$30–$45
$$$$	$45–$60
$$$$$	over $60

Spaghetti Junction

TOP 10 Restaurants

1 Garden Restaurant
Surrounded by gardens, this alfresco restaurant may serve rack of lamb with fresh mint. Save room for the sinful chocolate swirl cheesecake. ✪ *Long Bay Beach Resort, North Coast Rd, Long Bay* • *284-495-4252* • *No lunch* • *$$$$*

2 Sugar Mill Restaurant
Look for sautéed scallops with a ginger lime sauce or flying fish tempura in this lovely restaurant *(see p31)*. ✪ *North Coast Rd, Apple Bay* • *284-495-4355* • *www.sugarmillhotel.com* • *No lunch* • *$$$$*

3 Skyworld
Go for the view but stay for the food, including the filet mignon in a cranberry and tequila sauce *(see p33)*. ✪ *Ridge Road, Joe's Hill* • *284-494-3567* • *$$$$*

4 Captain's Table
Pick your own lobster right from the pool or dine on fresh local fish grilled Cajun style or drizzled with a spicy sauce. Meat-eaters can opt for lamb and filet mignon. ✪ *Wickhams Cay I, Road Town* • *284-494-3885* • *$$$$*

5 Spaghetti Junction
Local favorite famous for its shrimp, scallops, and lobster in a tomato, basil, and lemon cream sauce. ✪ *Wickhams Cay I, Road Town* • *284-494-4880* • *No lunch* • *$$$*

6 Capriccio di Mare
You can make a meal out of appetizers such as the octopus salad and crostini with tomato and garlic here. ✪ *Waterfront Dr, Road Town* • *284-494-5369* • *$$$*

7 Le Cabanon
Casual French restaurant serving excellent food, such as monkfish in a chive butter sauce and fine cheeses. ✪ *Waterfront Dr, Road Town* • *284-494-8660* • *$$$$*

8 Pusser's Pub
The legendary rum drinks are the favorites at Pusser's *(see p35)*. It serves good pub grub including fish and chips, burgers, and pizzas. ✪ *Main St, Road Town* • *284-494-3897* • *$$$*

9 Brandywine Bay
This elegant place serves superb Italian fare *(see p31)*. The menu changes often, but look for the grilled veal chops with ricotta and sun-dried tomatoes. ✪ *Sir Francis Drake Hwy, Brandywine Bay* • *284-495-2301* • *No lunch* • *$$$$*

10 Eclipse
Delicious fresh swordfish and spicy curries served on the waterfront. ✪ *Fat Hogs Bay, East End* • *284-495-1646* • *No lunch* • *$$$$*

Following pages **Three Kings Day celebration, St. Croix Christmas Festival, Christiansted**

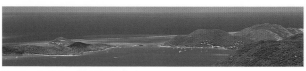

View from North Sound Road, Virgin Gorda

Virgin Gorda & the Outer Islands

THICKLY FORESTED VIRGIN GORDA punctuates the string of volcanic islands that make up the USVI and BVI. Named the "Fat Virgin" by Christopher Columbus, the 8.5-sq mile (22-sq km) island with 3,000 inhabitants is the most populous of the 60 or so outer islands. Anegada sits 15 miles (24 km) to its east, a flat atoll fringed by a spectacular reef and home to only 173 hearty souls. Jost Van Dyke, to the west of Tortola, has 200 folks on its 3 sq miles (8 sq km). Many other islands are occupied by exclusive hotels and private homes. The rest are unpopulated, waiting for sailors to drop anchor at their harbors. Except for Virgin Gorda, access is difficult. But if you want some peace on a truly tropical idyll, it's well worth the effort.

🔟 Sights

1. Spanish Town, Virgin Gorda
2. Spring Bay Beach, Virgin Gorda
3. Savannah Bay, Virgin Gorda
4. North Sound, Virgin Gorda
5. Anegada Beaches
6. Marina Cay
7. Salt Island
8. Norman Island
9. Jost Van Dyke
10. Sandy Cay

Spring Bay Beach

For more on the BVI outer islands See pp21, 22–3, 25

Ferry port, Spanish Town, Virgin Gorda

1 Spanish Town, Virgin Gorda

The heart of Virgin Gorda's commerce and transportation, Spanish Town is squeezed between the Atlantic and the Caribbean Sea. Most of its shops and restaurants are housed at Virgin Gorda Yacht Harbor. Lively Lee Road bisects the west side of town, with the tiny strip of an airport on the east. The ferry dock sits a short walk from Yacht Harbor. Residents often refer to Spanish Town as The Valley, but that is in fact the name of the island's southern part. ⊗ Map L4

2 Spring Bay Beach, Virgin Gorda

Very close to the busy Baths National Park (see p21), the white, sandy Spring Bay Beach provides a peaceful respite worth the five-minute walk from the road. Pretty natural pools created by huge boulders provide perfect swimming and snorkeling. Swings and picnic tables on a grassy lawn get you

out of the sand. You'll find a few restaurants at the nearby Baths and along the 10-minute drive to Spanish Town. ⊗ Map L4

3 Savannah Bay, Virgin Gorda

Breathtaking is the best word to use when describing this lengthy stretch of luscious white sand. The hillside overlook, just as you start down toward the beach entrance, provides terrific photo opportunities for shutterbugs. Pack a picnic lunch and bring plenty of water and sunscreen, as there are no facilities. While it's easy to reach and just a short drive from Spanish Town, the beach sees few visitors.
⊗ Map L4 • North Sound Rd

4 North Sound, Virgin Gorda

A handful of small resorts fringe North Sound's shoreline. Most are reached only by complimentary boat service from Gun Creek or in the case of Biras Creek Resort, from Beef Island (see p83). The majority welcome day visitors to their restaurants and shops. Protected North Sound serves as one of the BVI's hottest sailing destinations. Sailors on week-long charters out of Tortola and the USVI drop anchor here and head for the easy camaraderie of the bars. ⊗ Map M3

Savannah Bay, Virgin Gorda

Island-Hopping the Local Way

To the uninitiated, inter-island ferry travel in the BVI's outer islands *(see p96)* can be very confusing. There are usually no signs or ticket booths and crews are often reluctant to part with information. Ask people waiting for the ferries for directions. You'll see all manner of objects on board – refrigerators may sit cheek-by-jowl with a big dog on his way home from the veterinarian.

5 Anegada Beaches

Spectacular white sand beaches, providing superb sunning and snorkeling, rim this 15-sq mile (39-sq km) atoll. The reef fringing the island keeps the waters calm and the fish plentiful. Some beaches have fanciful names such as Cow Wreck, so named because a ship full of bones destined to become buttons washed up on the reef. Casual restaurants serving seafood and more sit along the sands, well back from the water.

6 Marina Cay

This island served as the setting for *Two on the Isle*, a 1960s movie starring Sidney Poitier and John Cassavetes, which was based on a 1930s book by Robb White. The 8-acre Marina Cay is now home to a Pusser's Hotel and Restaurant *(see p116)*. Take the complimentary ferry from Trellis Bay, Tortola, and spend a day visiting the bar and the beaches, snorkeling, or taking a stroll around the island. The home White built has been restored as a reading room and book exchange. ✎ *Map J4*

7 Salt Island

Islanders still harvest salt from the three natural ponds that dot this tiny cay. You're welcome to come ashore to inspect the salt ponds, stroll the beach, and enjoy the solitude. A popular dive site, the Wreck of the Rhone National Park sits just offshore. The *Rhone*, a 310-ft (94-m) royal mail ship, split in two when it hit Salt Island during an 1867 hurricane. The captain and most of the crew perished. ✎ *Map J5*

8 Norman Island

A mostly unpopulated island, Norman Island was reputedly the setting for Robert Louis Stevenson's book *Treasure Island*. The island's main harbor, the Bight, draws sailors to its Pirates Bight, a bar and restaurant located on the beach, and the floating William Thornton bar and restaurant. Around the Bight

Marina Cay

The Wreck of the Rhone was used to film the 1976 movie, The Deep, *starring Jacqueline Bisset and Nick Nolte*

Norman Island

sits a series of caves that make for great snorkeling. The anchorage can get busy with dinghies going to and fro, so be careful while in the water. ◈ *Map H6*

9 Jost Van Dyke
Home to a handful of hoppin' bars, some guesthouses, and a few small stores sitting along its sandy lanes, Great Harbour is the island's main settlement. If you're sailing and haven't cleared Immigration in Tortola, visit the BVI Customs and Immigration office on the waterfront. If you want a change of scene, take a stroll west to White Bay, the next bay over and home to Sandcastle hotel and restaurant (see p114). Head off to the east to Little Harbour, which offers more bars and restaurants. ◈ *Map G3*

10 Sandy Cay
An unpopulated speck off Jost Van Dyke perfect for those who love solitude, Sandy Cay is ringed with a desert-island style beach. With no protected harbor, it is best used during the winter season as a day sailboat anchorage or stopping spot for power boats. When calmer summer weather arrives, it makes a fine overnight halt. Swim in limpid water, sun on the gorgeous white beach, and stroll through the greenery that covers the interior of the island. ◈ *Map H3*

Bar-Crawling in North Sound, Virgin Gorda

Late Afternoon

⏰ Since you'll want your stomach well-lined before starting a busy night, head for the Bitter End Yacht Club's **Clubhouse Steak & Seafood Grille** (see p93) for sundowners and then dinner. To get there, park your car at Gun Creek, located at the end of a steep downhill road in North Sound, and take the complimentary ferry.

Evening

Drop in for after-dinner drinks and dancing at **Saba Rock Resort** (see p116), just a 200-yard (180-m) boat trip away from Bitter End Yacht Club. Call them at 284-495-7711 or VHF 16 for a ride.

Get back to Bitter End Yacht Club, to wind down at **The English Pub**. This bar stays open till very late, but remember that the last ferry to Gun Creek departs at 10 pm.

Later

If you have any energy left, stop by **The Restaurant at Leverick Bay** (see p93), located a short drive shoreside in North Sound, for a nightcap or cup of coffee.

Make sure someone in your group abstains from drinking throughout. On your drive back to the hotel, the twisting roads can be treacherous with a few drinks down the hatch.

Saba Rock Resort often closes in September and other places may have shorter hours during the summer and fall. Always do a last-minute check of opening and closing hours.

Left **Learning to sail at the Bitter End Yacht Club** Right **Kayak**

10 Outdoor Activities

1 Boating, Virgin Gorda
While hotels organize day sails, most folks prefer to rent small sail or power boats for a trip around North Sound on their own. ⊗ Map M3 • Leverick Bay Watersports, North Sound • 284-495-7376 • www.watersportsbvi.com

2 Learn to Sail, Virgin Gorda
The Bitter End Yacht Club in Virgin Gorda has a 3-day program that gets you ready to handle bare boats. ⊗ Map M3 • Bitter End Yacht Club, North Sound • 800-872-2392, 284-494-2746 • www.beyc.com

3 Windsurfing, Virgin Gorda
Zip across the protected waters of Virgin Gorda's North Sound on a windsurfer rented from Bitter End Yacht Club (see above for details).

4 Fishing, Anegada
Go bonefishing in Anegada's fringing reef with Garfield's Guides. ⊗ 284-495-9569

5 Flamingo Watching, Anegada
The island's salt ponds are the only places in the USVI and BVI where pink flamingos roost. Look, but do not disturb. ⊗ Map K1

6 Hiking
For great views from the top of Virgin Gorda's Gorda Peak, take the 15-minute hike off North Sound Road. Many outer islands have trails leading to their peaks.

7 Kayaking
Most hotels in Virgin Gorda and the outer islands provide free kayaks. If not, rent one at Virgin Gorda's Leverick Bay Watersports (see No. 1 for details).

8 Scuba
Hotels arrange scuba trips for their guests if they don't provide this activity at their watersports center. Otherwise, sign up for a trip with Dive BVI at Leverick Bay or Virgin Gorda Yacht Harbor. ⊗ Map M3, L4 • Dive BVI • 284-495-5513 • www.divebvi.com

9 Snorkeling
With pristine waters and deserted beaches, this region provides some of the world's best snorkeling. At Flash of Beauty in Loblolly Bay, Anegada, dive down to explore caves. ⊗ Map M1

10 Swimming
You'll be continually tempted to dunk in the crystal clear sea that surrounds Virgin Gorda and the outer islands. Savannah Bay and the Baths (see p23) in Virgin Gorda especially provide fantastic swimming.

Snorkeling in the Baths, Virgin Gorda

Price Categories

For a three-course
meal for one with half
a bottle of wine (or
equivalent meal), taxes,
and extra charges.

$	under $20
$$	$20–$30
$$$	$30–$45
$$$$	$45–$60
$$$$$	over $60

William Thornton floating restaurant, Norman Island

🖫10 Restaurants

1 Clubhouse Steak & Seafood Grille, Virgin Gorda

Hop the complimentary ferry to the Bitter End Yacht Club's breezy restaurant, where the meal includes appetizer, soup, entrée, dessert, and an after-dinner rum. The tropical fruit tart is delicious. ⊗ *Bitter End Yacht Club, North Sound • 284-494-2746 • $$$*

2 The Restaurant at Leverick Bay, Virgin Gorda

Enjoy charbroiled grouper or pasta primavera with shrimp while sitting dockside at Leverick Bay Resort. ⊗ *Leverick Bay Rd, North Sound • 284-495-7154 • $$$$*

3 The Dog & Dolphin, Virgin Gorda

Try an island treat, the flaky red snapper and baked fresh vegetables, at this poolside place. ⊗ *Nail Bay Resort, Off North Sound Rd • 284-494-8000 • $$$$*

4 The Rock Café, Virgin Gorda

Nestled among big boulders, the eclectic Rock Café serves pasta, grilled fish, and pizza with equal flair. ⊗ *Tower Rd • 284-495-5482 • No lunch • $$$$*

5 Top of the Baths, Virgin Gorda

This casual restaurant serves excellent West Indian and continental fare. Go for the tender conch in curry sauce. ⊗ *Tower Rd • 284-495-5497 • $$$$$*

6 Anegada Reef Hotel

Lobster served in many forms is the thing at this beach-front restaurant. If you're there for lunch, opt for the lobster salad sandwich on a soft roll. ⊗ *Map K1 • Setting Point • 284-495-8002 • $$$$$*

7 Cow Wreck Beach Bar & Grill, Anegada

Fresh Anegada lobster served in the shell and dripping butter is the dish to order here. ⊗ *Map K1 • Cow Wreck Bay • 284-495-8047 • $$$$$*

8 Cooper Island Beach Club

Dine under the stars on the patio with the sea close by. ⊗ *Map K5 • Call on VHF Channel 16 • $$$*

9 William Thornton, Norman Island

This popular converted lumber schooner serves yummy fare. ⊗ *Map H6 • Call on VHF Channel 16 • $$$*

10 Foxy's, Jost Van Dyke

Foxy Callwood just might make up a song about you while you're dining *(see p37)*. ⊗ *Map G3 • Great Harbour • 284-495-9258 • $$$$*

You need your own boat or a chartered one to get to the restaurants on the smaller islands

STREETSMART

VIRGIN ISLANDS' TOP 10

Left **Airport at St. Thomas** Center **Seaplane at Charlotte Amalie** Right **Ferry at Red Hook**

Arriving in the Virgin Islands

1 Getting There
Major airlines fly direct to St. Thomas and St. Croix from airports on the US mainland. Or you can fly into these islands, and also Virgin Gorda and Tortola, from the US, Europe, or South America via San Juan, Puerto Rico. Anegada can be reached from St. Thomas via Tortola. There are no flights to St. John; it's reached via ferry from St. Thomas.

2 Airfares
Airfares vary widely, depending on season and sales. Doublecheck with the airline, Internet suppliers, and your travel agent to find the best price. Some wholesalers offer great airfare and hotel packages.

3 Henry E. Rohlsen Airport, St. Croix
An international airport near the western end of St. Croix near Frederiksted, this has a casual restaurant, a few shops, and rental car agencies. Flights arrive here from the US mainland and other Caribbean Islands.

4 Cyril E. King Airport, St. Thomas
Several hotels sit near this international airport, which is a 10-minute ride from Charlotte Amalie and about a half-hour ride away from Red Hook. It has a small restaurant, a gift shop, and rental car agencies.

5 Terrance B. Lettsome International Airport, Beef Island, Tortola
The airport handles only smaller planes arriving from San Juan, St. Thomas, and other Caribbean Islands. If you're stranded here, you can browse the few small shops or take the free ferry to Pusser's Restaurant on nearby Marina Cay (see p90).

6 Airports in Virgin Gorda & Anegada
With its Band Aid-sized runway, Virgin Gorda's airport is on the ramshackle side, but that's part of the charm of arriving here. Procedures are casual, too. A shack at the edge of the tiny runway, Anegada's Auguste George International Airport is served only by Clair Aero and charter flights.

7 Seaplane
Island-hopping is fairly easy with Seaborne Airlines' flights between in-town waterfront locations in Charlotte Amalie, St. Thomas, and Christiansted and Frederiksted, St. Croix. Midday rates are lower.

8 USVI to Tortola Ferries
Ferries connect Charlotte Amalie and Red Hook on St. Thomas with West End and Road Town on Tortola. From Cruz Bay, St. John, you can catch a ferry to West End.

9 Ferries to Virgin Gorda & the Outer Islands
Ferry connections (on the unreliable side) link Charlotte Amalie, Road Town, and Cruz Bay to Virgin Gorda, and to Jost Van Dyke from West End and Cruz Bay. Hotels on the outer islands and in remote locations run their own ferries from Tortola (see also p90).

10 St. Thomas to St. John Ferries
Ferries shunt between Red Hook, St. Thomas, and Cruz Bay, St. John, on the hour. There are also round trips to Cruz Bay from Charlotte Amalie several times a day.

Directory

Airlines
- American Airlines & American Eagle: 800-874-4884; www.aa.com
- Delta Airlines: 800-221-1212; www.delta.com
- US Airways: 800-622-1015; www.usairways.com
- Seaborne Airlines 340-773-6442; www.seaborneairlines.com

Airports
- Henry E. Rohlsen: 340-778-1012
- Cyril E. King: 340-774-5100
- Terrance B. Lettsome: 284-495-2525

Ferry Services
- www.usvitourism.vi
- www.bvitouristboard.com

Previous pages **Havensight pier, St. Thomas**

Left **Taxis, Virgin Gorda** Center **Keep Left armband** Right **Bus Stop sign, Cruz Bay, St. John**

10 Getting Around

1 Taxis
Taxi drivers in both the USVI and BVI are of two types – helpful or shockingly rude. Taxis are plentiful at airports, docks, and hotels on the more populated islands. If you plan to go off the beaten path, ask your hotel or villa manager to line up a taxi. It's pointless to argue about overcharging – chalk it up to the cost of vacationing.

2 Car Rentals
A few brand names such as Hertz and Avis operate in St. Thomas, St. Croix, Tortola, and Virgin Gorda, but most car rentals are local companies. Ask your hotel for recommendations. It's best to reserve before you travel. Rates are high.

3 Types of Vehicles
Get a vehicle with four-wheel drive and high clearance to drive on the dirt roads. Visitors to more populated islands should ensure their vehicles have a hard top and locks to prevent theft.

4 Motorscooters
Motorscooter rentals seem to come and go, particularly on St. John, but in general they're a bad idea. Traffic moves at a good clip and sudden rain showers make for slippery roads, both creating conditions that can lead to accidents. Don't be tempted by a price lower than a rental car.

5 Rules of the Road
Drivers in both the USVI and BVI drive on the left side of the road in left-hand drive vehicles. On all islands, drivers are prone to stop for a chat with someone walking along the road, causing dangerous traffic conditions as impatient motorists try to pass on a curve. Use caution.

6 Road Conditions
Roads range from a major highway in St. Croix to sandy tracks in Anegada, with every permutation in between. The roads on the mountainous islands twist and turn. On the more populated islands, the main roads and many secondary roads are paved, but you'll find dirt roads everywhere.

7 Driver's Licenses
While your current driver's license will do to rent and drive a vehicle in the USVI, the BVI requires that all visiting drivers also purchase a temporary BVI license, available at all car rental agencies – you must present your regular driver's license for this.

8 Buses
The USVI has VITRAN buses, though the service is unreliable in St. Croix and St. Thomas. For patient folks, they're a good way to sightsee at minimal cost. BVI has no public bus service.

9 Hitchhiking
Hitchhiking is an accepted way to get around in the USVI and BVI, but think twice about it in St. Thomas and St. Croix. It's a bit safer on other islands, but use caution. Stick out your forefinger to indicate you want a ride, pointing in the direction you wish to go.

10 Addresses
Addresses in both the USVI and BVI are horribly confusing. In Charlotte Amalie and Christiansted, the buildings have numbers that often don't make sense. Out in the country, it's even worse. Make sure you have a map and written directions.

Directory

Car Rentals
• Avis: St. Croix 340-778-9355; St. Thomas 340-774-1468; Tortola 284-494-3322
• Hertz: St. Croix 340-778-1402; St. Thomas 340-774-1879; Tortola 284-495-2763
• St. John Car Rental: 340-776-6103
• L&S Jeep Rental, Virgin Gorda: 284-495-5297

Bus Services
• St. Croix: 340-778-0898
• St. John: 340-774-0165
• St. Thomas: 340-776-4844

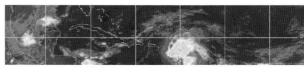

Infrared satellite image of Hurricane Jose, taken on October 20, 1999

🔟 General Information

1 When to Go
The islands are a year-round destination, though more visitors come in winter than in summer. Daytime temperatures run in the low to mid-80s (27°C) in winter, with the summer months about 10 degrees (12°C) higher. It can rain at any time of the year.

2 Hurricane Season
Although hurricane season officially runs June 1 to November 30, it starts to ramp up in mid-August, reaching its peak in mid-September. The weather can be quite hot at that time. Hotel rates are temptingly low during this season, but you may have to cut your vacation short if a hurricane threatens.

3 USVI: Passports & Visas
US citizens can enter the USVI without a passport and stay as long as they like, but they need to show a passport, voter's registration card, or birth certificate when they leave. Citizens of some countries such as the UK need a passport but no visa for up to three months. Check the US State Department's website for information.

4 BVI: Passports & Visas
In theory, Canadian and US citizens only need a birth certificate to enter the BVI, but in practice,

the Immigration officers prefer a passport from everyone including British citizens. Stays of over a month require a visa. Visitors from some countries need a visa for entry.

5 USVI: Customs & Immigration
You do not have to clear Customs and Immigration on flights into the USVI from the US mainland and Puerto Rico, but you will when departing. Passengers arriving on flights or ferry boats from Caribbean countries, including the BVI, must clear in. Fruit may be confiscated when arriving from Caribbean countries or when departing for the US.

6 BVI: Customs & Immigration
All arriving airline and ferry passengers except for those coming from other islands in the BVI must clear in. You may be questioned at Customs about objects such as cameras and computers.

7 Language
Most USVI and BVI residents born in the Caribbean speak standard English with a distinctive accent, as well as their native English Creole. It can sometimes be difficult to understand them, but don't be shy about asking them in a friendly way to repeat what they have said. Keep in mind that they

may have trouble understanding you as well.

8 Time Zone
The USVI and BVI are on Atlantic Standard Time (GMT –4). In winter, this puts them an hour ahead of Eastern Standard Time, but when the US goes on Daylight Saving Time, the USVI and BVI do not change. This means that in summer, island time is the same as on the US East Coast.

9 Departure Tax
There is no departure tax from the USVI, but the BVI charges $10 per person for airline passengers, $5 per person for boat passengers, and $10 per person for cruise ship passengers. This fee is often included in your fare when traveling on a cruise or with a group.

10 Etiquette
Although most restaurants are alfresco, some have no smoking sections. The legal age for drinking in the USVI is 18; it is 16 in the BVI. Enforcement varies, but if you look younger than those ages, be prepared to show identification.

Visa Information

USVI Visas
• www.travel.state.gov/visa_services

BVI Visas
• www.bvitouristboard.com

Left **Local kids** Right **Nazareth Lutheran Church, Cruz Bay**

Facts & Figures

1 Population
The USVI officially has 108,612 inhabitants, with 53,234 on St. Croix, 51,181 on St. Thomas, and 4,197 on St. John. The total count of people in the BVI is 20,988, with 17,233 on Tortola. Virgin Gorda has 3,174 inhabitants, Jost Van Dyke 211, and Anegada 182. The rest of the 188 people are scattered about on small cays and boats.

2 Racial Distribution
The majority of USVI and BVI residents are black descendents of slaves brought over from West Africa. Only in St. John does the number of white residents approach that of black. The Hispanic population is fairly large in St. Croix, and is growing on other islands through immigration.

3 Political Status
The USVI is an Unincorporated Territory of the US. Its residents are US citizens, but cannot vote in presidential elections. The BVI is a Crown Colony of the UK. Its residents are British citizens, but may only vote locally.

4 USVI Congressional Representation
USVI voters elect a delegate to the US House of Representatives. She has no vote in either congressional committees or on the floor, but does lobby for federal funding for the territory. She has offices in Washington, St. Croix, and St. Thomas. The USVI is considered one district. It has no representative in the US Senate.

5 Island Top Officials
Every four years, USVI voters elect a governor and lieutenant governor. They also elect a 15-member one-house Legislature every two years. In the BVI, voters elect a 13-member unicameral Legislative Council every four years. The Queen appoints the BVI governor, who in turn appoints the chief minister from among the members of the Legislative Council.

6 Local Government
In the USVI, the governor appoints his cabinet members, who head different departments. Several semi-autonomous agencies oversee power and water generation, the ports and airports, and the university. In the BVI, members of the Legislative Council appointed to the cabinet by the governor oversee the various departments.

7 Churches & Synagogues
There are churches at nearly every bend in the road in the VI. Many are mainline denominations such as Anglican, Catholic, and Moravian, but there are an increasing number of evangelical churches with no denominational affiliation. St. Thomas has a synagogue (see p17). Visitors are welcome at religious services, but wear your Sunday finery.

8 BVI Economy
While tourism is a mainstay and the most visible part of the islands' economy, the BVI's huge offshore banking industry is equally important. A total of 51,697 companies are registered in the BVI, but most of them merely funnel their paperwork through small Tortola-based companies set up to deal with multitudes of companies.

9 USVI Economy
Tourism is the heart of the USVI economy, although St. Croix does have the huge Hovensa oil refinery that employs more workers than any other private company. The island also has a few watch factories and a rum factory.

10 Tourism
More tourists visit both the USVI and BVI in winter. However, both can be visited year-round. The USVI sees 2.3 million visitors a year, with 2.2 million of them visiting St. Thomas/St. John. In the BVI, the vast majority of the 535,002 tourists visit Tortola.

Left **Tourist information kiosk, USVI** Center **BVI Tourism Board sign** Right *St. John Guidebook*

🔟 Sources of Information

1 USVI Tourist Board
The government has offices in large cities across the US and in Canada, England, and Denmark. Call up or check the official website for access to information.

2 BVI Tourist Board
The BVI Tourist Board has a few offices scattered across Europe and the US, but the fastest way to get information is to call up the info line or access the Board's comprehensive website, which features some useful articles under BVIslands Magazine.

3 Caribbean Vacation Planner
Check out this slick book of the Caribbean Tourism Organization. Its website is very useful; it provides an excellent overview of the Caribbean chain and specifics on each island as well as the latest on deals and events.

4 Travel Talk On-line
Visit this website to ask questions and find out what other folks have to say about your intended holiday destination. Easy to use, the website has useful information and a pleasant tone.

5 St. Croix This Week
This free publication with its familiar pink cover is chock full of information and advertisements about St. Croix. You can find it at the airport, hotels, tourism offices, and other places. Subscriptions are available.

6 St. John Guidebook
With cartoons as well as the requisite advertisements, this small booklet provides a humorous insight into St. John life. Pick up a free copy at the Cruz Bay ferry dock or the tourism office, or order by mail. The online version isn't nearly as funny.

7 St. Thomas/St. John This Week
The granddaddy of all USVI and BVI tourism magazines, this free magazine with its well-known yellow cover is filled with information and advertisements about St. Thomas and St. John. Get a copy at the airport and numerous locations in the islands. You can also subscribe.

8 The BVI Welcome
This classy free publication, available at various locations, comes out every other month. In addition to the usual advertisements, it has articles on current events. The magazine's website is also very helpful. Subscriptions to the US are $25 a year.

9 Bookstores
Find books about the USVI and BVI at gift shops and bookstores in St. Thomas and St. Croix.

10 The Weather Channel
Cable television channels in the USVI and BVI carry this useful station with its frequent updates on local weather. Its Tropical Weather update at 10 minutes to the hour during the hurricane season is especially helpful.

Directory

Tourist Boards
- USVI Tourist Board: www.usvitourism.vi
- BVI Tourist Board: www.bvitouristboard.com

Magazines/Websites
- Caribbean Vacation Planner: www.doitcaribbean.com
- Travel Talk On-line: www.traveltalkonline.com
- St. Croix This Week: www.stcroixthisweek.com
- St. John Guidebook: www.stjohnguidebook.com
- St. Thomas/St. John This Week: www.stthomasthisweek.com
- The BVI Welcome: www.bviwelcome.com

Bookstores
- Dockside Books, Havensight Mall, St. Thomas
- Undercover Books, Gallows Bay Shopping Center, St. Croix

  Surfing will turn up dozens of unofficial websites with useful information on both the USVI and BVI

Left **ATM, Cruz Bay, St. John** Center **Stamp, BVI** Right **Internet access sign, St. John**

TOP 10 Banking & Communications

1 Money
Both the USVI and BVI use US currency. US dollars were introduced in the BVI in the mid-20th century, when BVIers went to nearby USVI to work. This led them to abandon the barter system previously in use. The US dollar became legal tender in the BVI in 1959.

2 Changing Money
Changing foreign currency is difficult. Only Scotia Bank branches in St. Croix, St. John, St. Thomas, and Tortola will exchange small amounts of some currencies. You must show identification. It's easier to change money into US dollars before you leave home or in major airports.

3 Credit Cards & Traveler's Checks
Most shops, restaurants, car rental companies, attractions, and hotels take credit cards, but in the outer BVIs you may find an occasional one that doesn't. Traveler's checks are usually accepted, but small businesses may not be able to make change for large denominations.

4 ATMs
ATMs accept cards from most systems, but there is usually a charge. Find ATMs at banks and supermarkets in St. Croix, St. John, St. Thomas, and Tortola. Outer BVI islands do not have banks.

5 Post Offices
Except for the tiniest islands in the BVI, all USVI and BVI islands have post offices. Outer island hotels often have boxes at the front desk to drop off your postcards home. Don't expect speedy delivery.

6 Cell Phones
Some systems work, some don't. Even if your home cell phone company claims their phone will work in the USVI and BVI, don't count on it. Your chances are better in the USVI if you have a US company such as Cingular Wireless. In the BVI, you may get lucky if you phone from high elevations or along the coast.

7 Pay Phones
You'll find pay phones on most islands. Most phones charge 25 cents, but some privately owned phones are 35 cents. A phone card, available at pharmacies, department stores, and gift shops, is your best bet for making long distance calls. BVI phones only use phone cards bought in the BVI.

8 Internet
Many larger hotels provide complimentary Internet service at their business center. Check with your own Internet Service Provider if they have a number to use in the islands. Otherwise, you're faced with long-distance charges from the USVI and in the BVI, with paying international phone rates.

9 Newspapers
Catch up with international events as well as USVI news by reading the *Daily News* and *St. Croix Avis* in St. Croix and St. Thomas. St. John has two papers, the *St. John Times* and *Tradewinds*, both carrying local news. In the BVI, read local news in the *Beacon*, *Island Sun*, and the *BVI Standpoint*.

10 Television/Radio
While most hotels in the USVI and Tortola have at least a basic cable television service, those in Virgin Gorda and the outer islands may not. Hotels without television service may provide a VCR to watch movies. In a car, you'll have a choice of radio stations playing everything from reggae to classical.

Directory

Scotia Bank
• USVI: 340-774-0037
• BVI: 284-494-2526

International Codes
• Dialing USVI & BVI from overseas: USVI +1-340, BVI +1-284, then local number
• Dialing overseas from USVI & BVI: 011, then country code, area code & local number

---

 Visa and Mastercard are the most common credit cards here, but some places also take Discover and American Express

Left **Insect repellent** Center **Carrying an umbrella** Right **Hospital sign**

Surviving the Tropics

1 Sunburn
Slather on sunscreen to prevent sunburn. The tropical sun burns brightest between 10am and 2pm, so try and keep in the shade during those hours. Wear a hat, lightweight long-sleeved shirts, and long pants, and remember to keep your feet covered.

2 Bugs
Bugs are a fact of life in the tropics. While larger hotels annihilate bug populations with chemical sprays, you won't find that so everywhere. After a few days of rain, the mosquitoes come out. A nifty device, called a mosquito whacker, found at hardware stores and supermarkets, is quite handy.

3 Rain
Brief showers occur quite often, but occasionally you can get deluges that last for days. While this can put a damper on your vacation, it helps keep the island green. Carry an umbrella and bring some good books to while away the rainy hours.

4 Hospitals
Roy L. Schneider Hospital in St. Thomas and Juan F. Luis Hospital in St. Croix are the best equipped and can handle everything from heart attacks to broken legs. Tortola has Peebles Hospital. St. John, Virgin Gorda, Jost Van Dyke, and Anegada all have small clinics, but serious cases go by air or ferry to the hospitals.

5 Doctors
You will find qualified doctors in both the USVI and BVI, but it's a matter of luck. Ask your hotel for their recommendations. Some hotels have affiliations with doctors they trust.

6 Hyperbaric Chamber
Roy L. Schneider Hospital in St. Thomas has the only hyperbaric, or decompression, chamber in the USVI and BVI. The chamber helps divers who have got the bends to decompress. A spell in the chamber takes the excess nitrogen out of the diver's blood. Without the chamber, the bends can be painful, and sometimes fatal.

7 Pharmacies
Find full service pharmacies in St. Croix, St. John, St. Thomas, Tortola, and Virgin Gorda. While pharmacists will usually fill prescriptions issued outside the islands or will contact your doctor if necessary, your best bet is to come with a large enough supply to last throughout your stay. Prices at island pharmacies are usually higher than you'll find in other locations.

8 Dentists
Good dental care is available in the USVI and Tortola, but ask your hotel to recommend one. Dentists are usually willing to fit in emergency cases. If you are used to having the dentist bill your insurance company for dental procedures, you may have to pay upfront and submit a claim to the insurance company.

9 Electricity
Outlets in both the USVI and BVI produce 110 volts. However, power surges and outages are common even in well-developed areas. Use a surge protector for your computer. Larger hotels have generators that flip on automatically during outages, but at smaller properties you'll have to light candles. Bring a flashlight. When the power goes out, the toilet doesn't flush.

10 Water
Large hotels have reverse osmosis plants to desalinize sea water. The water is tested regularly to ensure its quality. Smaller hotels depend on cisterns to collect rainwater. The water may, or may not, go through a filtration system. If you're unsure, drink bottled water. Water may be in short supply, so you may be asked to limit your water usage.

In case of a serious illness, and if you are able to travel, head home should your insurance cover air ambulance service

Left **A hotel room safe** Center **Locking the trunk of a car** Right **Secluded beach**

🔟 Safety Tips

1 Avoid Unsafe Areas
St. Croix and St. Thomas have some areas that are decidedly unsafe for visitors even during daylight hours. Nighttime can also be problematic at some locations on the larger islands. Your hotel can advise you in both cases.

2 Use Hotel Room Safes
Larger hotels have room safes. Use them to protect your valuables while you're out of the room. It's worth the slight charge. Don't stash your wallet under the mattress or carry everything with you.

3 Don't Carry Drugs
It is illegal to possess or use non-prescription drugs such as marijuana, heroin, and cocaine in the USVI and BVI. Tourists are rarely approached to buy drugs, but it does happen. While enforcement is lax and penalties for simple possession are small, getting caught could ruin your vacation.

4 Avoid Assault
Vacationers are seldom robbery, assault, or murder victims, but it can occur. If you are accosted, hand over your wallet or jewelry before the criminal is tempted to use his gun. Call the police immediately. If you are a single woman, don't leave bars or parties with men you've just met.

5 Carry Minimal Cash
With few exceptions, credit cards are accepted all over the USVI and BVI. You will find automatic teller machines, called cash machines, at banks and in some stores. Traveler's checks are also accepted at many businesses. Therefore, keep cash in your pocket to a minimum so you won't tempt thieves.

6 Don't Leave Valuables on the Beach
It's easy for thieves to snatch your valuables while you're in the water or asleep. Leave your expensive camera locked in your hotel room safe. If you must carry it around, lock it in your vehicle trunk before you park at the beach.

7 Use Waterproof Containers
Buy a handy cylindrical container on a string to stash your cash, jewelry, and other small valuables while swimming. The container hangs around your neck for wearing in the water. Dive and gift shops carry these objects in the section with beach accessories.

8 Don't Leave Valuables in Sight in Your Vehicle
Thieves have tools to quickly open your vehicle. Even if you're only gone for a minute, you could return to find your stuff gone. Lock items in the trunk before entering the parking area. Thieves commonly watch parking lots at popular spots to look for ripe pickings.

9 Take Care on Deserted Beaches
Think twice before pulling over at that lovely deserted beach for a bit of solitude. On smaller islands, you'll be fine, but in places such as St. Croix and St. Thomas, you may be asking for trouble. Check with your hotel on beach safety.

10 Be Careful on Back Roads
In general, getting off the beaten path is perfectly safe as long as you use common sense. If an area looks unsavory, keep driving. Don't linger if a suspicious looking character approaches your car. Make sure your vehicle has enough gas when you start your exploring so you won't be stranded.

Emergency Phone Numbers

Ambulance, Fire & Police
- USVI 911
- BVI 999, 911

Boating Emergency
- USVI: US Coast Guard 340-776-3497
- BVI: Virgin Islands Search & Rescue 767, VHF Channel 16

Wedding aisle on the beach

TOP 10 Getting Married

1 Getting Married in the USVI

Apply for a marriage license at the Territorial Courts. The fee is $25 for the application and $35 for the license. You must wait eight days after the clerk receives the application. Licenses must be picked up in person.

2 Getting Married in the BVI

Apply in person for your license Monday through Friday at the Registrar's office in Tortola. The license costs $110. You must wait three days to get married. You'll need to arrange for banns to be published for three consecutive Sundays for a church wedding.

3 Officiates

In the USVI, a judge of the Territorial Court performs ceremonies at the court for $200. Clergy will officiate in a church. Most couples opt for a ceremony by a person certified by a non-denominational church and licensed by the government. In the BVI, only the registrar (who charges $135) or clergy can perform ceremonies.

4 Wedding Planner

Wedding planners help with finding a minister, rabbi, or registrar, hire reliable florists and musicians, and ensure a smooth ceremony. Many in the USVI are certified to perform ceremonies.

5 Packages

Many hotels offer packages that include the wedding ceremony and the honeymoon, and often have extras such as boat rides, and champagne dinners. Some places have packages that include accommodations for your wedding party and guests. Wedding planners also offer various packages.

6 Locations

Some people opt for a ceremony at one of the islands' small churches, but most head for the beach, a garden, or even a remote cay. Whim Plantation Museum and St. George Village Botanical Garden (see p58), both in St. Croix, make lovely wedding locations. Hotels with spacious grounds often have places set aside just for weddings.

7 Flowers

The bride's bouquet and groom's boutonnière are usually included in hotel or wedding planner packages. The islands' flora serves as a backdrop for your ceremony.

8 Photography

Your hotel or wedding planner will usually have a professional photographer on tap. Some packages include an album of photos sent later to your home, but many photographers give you the film to have developed at home.

9 Transportation

If you've always dreamed of arriving at your wedding ceremony in a stretch limousine, opt for a wedding in St. Thomas. Or you can drive yourself in a rental car to your informal ceremony at a beach or garden.

10 Music

You can hire a band if you're having a big shindig, but most couples have only a solo musician to entertain at their beach or garden ceremony. Your hotel or wedding planner will make recommendations if this does not come with your package.

Directory

License Authority
• St. Croix: Territorial Court Building, Kingshill; 340-778-9750
• St. Thomas: Territorial Court Building, Charlotte Amalie; 340-774-6680
• Tortola: Registrar's Office, Road Town; 284-494-3492

Wedding Planners
• St. Croix: Island Bride, www.island-bride.com
• St. John: Anne Marie Weddings, www.stjohnweddings.com
• St. Thomas: Weddings the Island Way, www.weddingstheislandway.com
• Tortola: BVI Wedding Planners & Consultants, www.bviweddings.com

Wedding planners, including those in charge of hotel wedding packages, can guide you through marriage license procedures

Left **Sandcastle on the Beach** Right **Wheelchair ramp at the Elaine I. Sprauve Library**

🔟 Visitors with Special Concerns

1 Gay & Lesbian Travelers
There are small gay and lesbian communities on most islands. Gay bars seem to come and go, so ask at your hotel. St. Croix has two beachfront resorts that cater to gay and lesbian visitors.

2 Seniors
Senior discounts are not common at Virgin Islands hotels and car rental agencies, but ask anyway. While ferry companies advertise senior fares, visitors are not eligible. Seniors worried about emergency medical care should stick to St. Croix and St. Thomas, which have hospitals.

3 Singles
Single vacationers can enjoy the busy bar scene on all islands. St. John's Virgin Islands National Park offers ranger-led hiking and snorkeling programs that draw a mix of visitors. Stay at small hotels or inns where the staff will make introductions.

4 Disabled Travelers
The situation is improving, but disabled visitors will not find uniform easy access. Some places have curb cuts, a few hotels offer rooms with wide doorways *(see Secret Harbour Beach Resort, p117)*, and some buildings have ramps, but these are rare cases.

5 Children
The islands are family friendly. Hotels offer kids' programs, there are many child-oriented attractions, and the beach is a great place for youngsters to let off steam. Spend Sunday at a popular beach to give your kids a chance to meet local children *(see pp38–9)*.

6 Babysitters
Many hotels and vacation villa managers have lists of reliable babysitters. Check at the front desk or concierge of your hotel or ask your villa manager. Rates vary by time of day and number of children.

7 Alcoholics & Drug Abusers
Alcoholics Anonymous, Narcotics Anonymous, and other self-help groups meet on most islands. Check local newspapers for meeting times and places or call up. Alcohol and drug abuse are serious problems in the islands, and these groups have helped many people. Visitors are welcome at meetings.

8 Pets
Dogs and cats can enter the USVI with health and rabies certificates from their home veterinarian. A local vet must issue the same certificates when leaving. In the BVI, you need an Agriculture Department import permit. You may have a huge surcharge added to your fare if you take your pet in a taxi.

9 Honeymooners
Both the USVI and BVI are honeymoon heavens, and many hotels offer special honeymoon packages. Palm-fringed beaches, starlight nights, intimate restaurants, and lazy days in a hammock promote romance, and some couples return year after year to celebrate their anniversary.

10 Rotarians
Many Rotary clubs meet weekly at restaurants throughout the USVI and BVI. Ask at your hotel for a meeting location near you. It'll give you a chance to meet the islands' influential people.

Directory

Gay & Lesbian Spots
• *Sandcastle on the Beach: 127 Smithfield, Frederiksted, St. Croix; 800-524-2018; www. sandcastleonthebeach. com*
• *The Cormorant Beach Club: La Grande Princesse, St. Croix; 800-4548-4460; www. cormorant-stcroix.com*

Self-help Groups
• *USVI: 340-776-5283*
• *BVI: 284-494-3125*

Agriculture Dept, BVI
284-495-2532

 Trunk Bay in St. John offers visitors a beach-friendly wheelchair free of charge

Left **A villa in the Salt River area, St. Croix** Right **Books at Marine Stores, Coral Bay, St. John**

TOP 10 Ways to Save Money

1 Carry Frozen Water

You can work up a major thirst in the hot tropical climate. If you have a refrigerator in your hotel room, do what islanders do – freeze bottles of water for use when you're out so you can drink the water as it melts. The bottles will sweat, so wrap in a washcloth and place in a plastic bag.

2 Pack a Picnic Lunch or Dinner

Instead of eating at the hotel's dining room, buy picnic fixings at the local supermarket. If you don't have a rental car, you may find a convenience store within walking distance of your hotel. Many hotels have their own convenience stores. Even if you must pay high prices at those stores, it's still cheaper than dining at a restaurant.

3 Rent a Condominium or Villa

Get more space plus save money by cooking meals when you rent a condominium or villa. Most come with a full set of kitchenware and gadgets. Even if local supermarket prices make you gasp, you'll still save money over eating out. Useful option when traveling with children.

4 Camp

If island hotel rates are out of your price range, trying camping.

The Cinnamon Bay Campground in St. John (see p119) gives you the best deal for renting a space if you bring your own tent. Campgrounds also rent tents already in place as well as cooking gear and coolers.

5 Shop at Supermarkets

You can pick up the ingredients for a full-course dinner complete with a dessert at the islands' supermarkets, but it's their take-out sections that tempt most vacationers. While the prices are on the high side, most supermarkets sell full dinners hot and ready for eating. Don't look for extensive salad bars such as those you'll find at many US supermarkets.

6 Take the Bus

The USVI's VITRAN bus service is slower than molasses, but it gives you an unusual look at the islands. Bus stops are marked along major roadways. Check with the driver to determine its destination. The bus is also a low-cost way to see the islands and to mingle with the locals. There is no regular bus service in the BVI.

7 Use the Book Exchange

Rather than trying to find a good read at gift shops and the bookstores in St. Thomas and St. Croix, ask around for a book

exchange at hotels and marinas. There's no requirement to leave a book when you take one, but they're a good place to get rid of the already read books you brought from home.

8 Bring Small Quantities of Staples from Home

Pack small amounts of coffee, tea bags, and spices in your luggage to avoid paying top dollar at island stores for larger quantities than you can consume during your trip.

9 Eat at Places with Early Bird Specials

A few restaurants have early bird specials, but you won't find the menu as extensive as later in the evening. However, you'll have plenty to pick from, the restaurant will be less crowded, and you'll have the rest of the evening to enjoy a stroll on the beach. Ask at your hotel for suggestions.

10 Go Before or After Hours at Beaches That Charge Admission

Trunk Bay in St. John and Magens Bay in St. Thomas charge a nominal admission fee, but if you have a family, the dollars add up. Wait until late afternoon, when the fee collector goes home, for a trip to the beach. In summer, you'll still have several hours of daylight to enjoy the beach.

Left **Formally dressed couple at Caneel Bay Resort, St. John** Right **Cows on Ridge Road, Tortola**

🔟 Local Quirks

1 Dress
Virgin Islanders put great store in appearances. Bathing suits are for the beach only. Even a cover-up over swimwear won't do for the islands' cities, towns, and shopping areas. Nudity is never allowed. You can get by with shorts and t-shirts at most casual restaurants, but more expensive places ask that you dress up a bit.

2 Manners
Remember to start your conversations with good morning, good afternoon, and good evening as the case may be. Islanders think such niceties are important. Hello and a smile doesn't quite do it. While folks are generally courteous to visitors, you may find some who go out of their way to be rude. Don't let it ruin your vacation.

3 Eye Contact & Handshakes
While you may be used to firmly grasping an extended hand and looking the other person square in the eye when saying hello, islanders may be more reserved. Handshakes are likely to be on the limp side and islanders almost never look you in the eye. Don't let this be a deterrent to making new friends.

4 Efficiency
While you do find pockets of efficiency, some procedures will leave you gasping at the convoluted way things are done. The heat adds to the general slowness. Things are improving as more and more companies get computers, but in the meantime, just adapt to the slow pace.

5 Holidays
Both the USVI and BVI celebrate the usual festivals, but there are dozens of others you've never heard of that merit days off. When Carnival, or whatever name a particular island uses to designate the event, happens, the entire place seems to shut down.

6 Roaming Animals
Look out for stray beasts while driving – cows, goats, horses, dogs, and cats all roam at will. The Agriculture Department is cracking down on this, but progress is slow. Dogs and cats dart through some restaurants looking for handouts, and a cat or two may come begging at your vacation villa.

7 Walk on the Left
While it's easy to see that vehicles use the left side of the road, sidewalk procedures are less obvious. Walk on the left to keep foot traffic flowing. In places swarming with tourists, you may find the situation a bit confused as visitors used to keeping right continue to do so while residents stick to their usual practice of keeping to the left.

8 Trash
Residents of both the USVI and BVI are just starting to catch on to the fact that trash strewn along the sides of the road looks unsightly. Yet, don't be surprised if you see a driver pitch a soda can out the window. They also throw out fruit skins, but that isn't as serious a problem as the tropical heat rots them quickly.

9 Treatment of Animals
Animal rights societies are making strides, but many people continue to mistreat animals of all sizes. Pit bulls and other aggressive dog breeds are extremely popular, but their owners train them with abuse. If you see what looks like a bad case of animal mishandling, call the police – don't get involved personally.

10 Loud Ambience
Tropical life plays out at top volume and with the windows open. If you dislike loud music, make sure your hotel or vacation villa isn't downwind of a place that has loud music until the wee hours. As for voice levels, what seems to be a heated argument between two islanders may merely be a casual conversation.

Streetsmart

Souvenirs at the Crafts Alive Village, Tortola

Shopping Tips

1 Bargaining

Bargaining usually only works at USVI and BVI markets or small stores where the proprietor serves as the salesclerk, but if you're buying in bulk or a slightly damaged item, it doesn't hurt to ask. Most prices in the USVI are already duty-free, as the sales people will be quick to point out when you ask for a discount.

2 Store Hours

Store hours vary, but most shops open at 9am or 10am. They usually close at around 5pm, but may stay open a bit later during the busier winter season. Most stores are closed Sundays and holidays except when cruise ships are in port. Stores near restaurants often stay open until around 9pm.

3 Carry Water

The tropics are hot, a lot hotter than you can imagine if you come from a cool climate. Even if you don't sweat, you're still at risk of dehydration. To shop healthy, carry a bottle of water and drink from it all the time. Residents know that you can keep going a lot longer if you regularly sip from a water bottle.

4 Wear Comfortable Shoes

While flimsy sandals look nice, shopping expeditions call for sturdy shoes. Sneakers with socks are fine. The socks help keep blisters at bay and soak up the sweat. If you don't like the idea of enclosed feet, consider sturdy sandals with thick soles. These will help you navigate the often uneven sidewalks in shopping areas.

5 Sales Tax

Shoppers pay no sales tax in the USVI and BVI. However, unseen taxes imposed by the governments abound. Store owners in the USVI pay a 4 percent gross receipts tax on all sales, and they pass that cost on to you. In the BVI, merchants must pay import duties, which again are ultimately paid by the customer.

6 Shop at Home First for High-priced Purchases

If you plan to buy an expensive camera or piece of pricey jewelry, check prices at home before you head to the USVI and BVI. Prices on those items can be lower in the USVI, thanks to the territory's duty-free status, but sometimes you can do better at your hometown discount or warehouse store or by shopping on the Internet.

7 Knockoffs

When shopping in places like Vendors Plaza in St. Thomas or at fairs and festivals, make sure that Gucci bag or Rolex watch is the real thing. While the government has clamped down on vendors selling knockoffs, it still happens sometimes. If the price looks too good to be true, it probably is.

8 Souvenirs

Both the USVI and BVI have numerous gift and jewelry stores to tempt you to part with big bucks. If you're looking for bargains, shop at discount stores such as Kmart, which carry calendars with island scenes and all sorts of bric-a-brac ideal for taking home.

9 Sales

Stores seldom have big blowout sales advertised in the local newspapers or sidewalk sale days. Instead, look for bargain racks, particularly on clothing and linen, during the summer and early fall months as stores strive to get rid of last year's merchandise.

10 Shipping

Many stores will ship your purchases nearly anywhere in the world for a fee. This makes sense for breakables, since the store assumes responsibility. If you want to do so yourself, ask for a box at a grocery store, buy tape, and head to the post office. Shipping to the US mainland is much cheaper in the USVI than the BVI.

Left **Plaza Extra supermarket, St. Croix** Right **Baskets of fruit, St. John**

TOP 10 Food & Drink

1 Supermarkets
Your best bets are the Plaza Extra stores in St. Croix and St. Thomas, Starfish Market in St. John, and Riteway or Bobby's in Tortola. Virgin Gorda has a few small grocery stores, including Buck's Food Market. The outer BVI islands don't have supermarkets.

2 Warehouse Stores
While the warehouse stores in St. Thomas and St. Croix pale in comparison to those found on the US mainland, they do sell items in bulk and often at lower prices than the supermarket. Cost-U-Less in these two islands has no membership fee.

3 Fresh Fruits & Vegetables
If you shop right after a shipment arrives, you may find crisp vegetables and fruit. But shipping takes its toll and, the farther you get from St. Thomas and St. Croix, the more wilted the produce. You can get local produce at roadside stands, but supply is erratic.

4 Delicatessen
Some supermarkets have delicatessen counters that whip up sandwiches to go. They often have take-out foods ideal for picnics or meals at your vacation abode.

5 Flexibility
If you're cooking at your condominium or vacation villa, don't fix your menu until you go shopping. Sometimes all the stores are out of an item that may be essential to your favorite dish.

6 Liquor Stores
Liquor is sold at duty-free prices in the USVI. Tourist areas have a few liquor stores, but you'll find a large selection and usually lower prices for common items such as gin at supermarkets and warehouse stores.

7 Convenience Stores
Convenience stores carrying snacks and basic staples are scattered around the larger islands. In the outer BVI islands, these stores are the main shopping spots; unless you want to use precious vacation time heading to the larger islands, you'll have to make do with them for your needs.

8 Take-out Stands
Gaily painted trucks sit along the roads on larger islands, stocked with all manner of West Indian food. A few have tables outside, but usually you'll have to take your lunch elsewhere to eat.

9 Getting Provisions for Yachts or Villas
If you are chartering a bare boat (see p22), the company will stock it with foods of your choosing. Your villa manager will usually do the same. This saves you time and possibly money since the provisioners often deal with wholesalers.

10 Private Chefs
Islands with large rosters of vacation villas have private chefs to cook tasty meals at your villa. They'll clean up as well. And they'll create just what you ordered.

Shop Addresses

Plaza Extra
• United Shopping Plaza, Queen Mary Hwy (Rte 70), Sion Farm, St. Croix; Map C5
• Tutu Park Mall, Rte 38, St. Thomas; Map C2

Starfish Market
Marketplace Shopping Center, Southside Rd (Rte 108), Cruz Bay, St. John; Map D2

Riteway
Between Main St & roundabout near Road Town, Tortola; Map H4

Bobby's
Wickhams Cay I near roundabout in Road Town, Tortola; Map H4

Buck's Food Market, VG Yacht Harbor, Spanish Town, VG; Map L4

Cost-U-Less
• Near Sunshine Mall, Queen Mary Hwy (Rte 70), St. Croix; Map B5
• Weymouth Rhymer Hwy (Rte 38), Donoe, St. Thomas; Map C2

If you're staying in a condominium or vacation villa in the USVI, shop for cases of beverages and snacks at warehouse stores

A couple on a terrace in a Tortola hotel

Accommodation Tips

1 Pick Your Location
Some islands have overall cheaper prices than others, with St. Croix having the lowest rates. You'll need to pay more for the privilege of staying on the beach on any island. A room with an ocean view is more expensive than one with a garden or city view, and in the few high-rise hotels, the top floors will probably cost you more.

2 Rates
Rates drop drastically around April 15 and go up again around December 15 when folks from colder climates escape to the tropics. Rates at some hotels are at their peak between Christmas and New Year. In the USVI, hotel rates are high in mid-February when schools on the US mainland close for the week that includes the national holiday, President's Day.

3 Deals
During the slower summer season, hotels often offer packages that include some meals and extras such as champagne, massages, day sails, scuba dives, and car rentals. They can be great deals if you take advantage of the extras.

4 Making Reservations
If you plan to visit during the busier winter season, it pays to book in advance if you're picky about where you stay. Reservations are essential if you are visiting a BVI outer island. Note that some hotels have mailing addresses on other islands.

5 Arriving Without Reservations
If you don't have a hotel reservation, call hotels from the airport or ferry terminal. You can check out the free tourist magazines and the hotel advertisements in those places. If you are taking a taxi, booking your room before you leave the airport is a must. Taxi drivers are usually unwilling to drive from hotel to hotel for you to find a room.

6 Tipping
In the USVI, tip between 15 and 20 percent in restaurants, depending on how pleased you are with the service. A service charge of anywhere from 10 to 15 percent is included at most BVI restaurants and hotels. A few USVI hotels also add a service charge. If they don't, leave the maid a few dollars a day depending on the service.

7 Phone Expenses
Some hotels charge for local phone calls and many charge for connecting to a long-distance carrier for credit card calls. Long-distance charges can be very high. You'll definitely save on long-distance calls if you use a phone card and the lobby phone. Read the information provided in your room or check at the front desk before you dial.

8 Parking
Most hotels have free parking, but it may not be next to your room. Parking in Charlotte Amalie, Christiansted, Cruz Bay, Road Town, and Spanish Town's Virgin Gorda Yacht Harbor can be very tight. Only Charlotte Amalie and Christiansted have paid parking lots where you can usually find a space.

9 Air Conditioning
Many hotels have air conditioning. However, smaller places and many vacation villas have windows open to the breeze. Unless your hotel room is in a pocket where the breezes don't blow or you prefer chilled air, you probably won't need to turn on the air conditioner.

10 Hotel Tax
Both the USVI and BVI tack a hotel occupancy tax onto your rate. In the USVI, you'll pay an additional 8 percent, and some St. John hoteliers also ask for a voluntary $1 a day donation. The St. John Accommodations Council uses the money to pay for good works. In the BVI, the hotel occupancy tax stands at 7 percent.

Check out the USVI Tourism Department's (see p100) summer promotions that offer gift certificates and discount coupons

Left **Villa at Mount Healthy, Tortola** Center **Villa Madeleine, St. Croix** Right **Villa in St. Croix**

TOP 10 Villa Management Companies

1 Caribbean Property Management, St. Croix

The owner Donna Ford and her capable staff manage about 25 villas with lovely views, ranging in size from two bedrooms to six, and a handful of condominium units. Most are on the island's East End, but the company has several at other locations. ☏ 800-496-7379 • www.enjoystcroix.com

2 Island Villas, St. Croix

While these villas are found all over St. Croix, most are on the East End, with great views from their locations up in the hills. One villa with seven bedrooms is perfect for family reunions. ☏ 800-626-4512 • www.stcroixislandvillas.com

3 Vacation St. Croix

Vacation St. Croix has more than two dozen luxury villas and condominiums, with beautiful views and furnishings. Most are in the Salt River area, but the company has a good handful on the island's East End. ☏ 877-788-0361 • www.vacationstx.com

4 Island Getaways, St. John

Long-time island resident Kathy McLaughlin looks after around 10 vacation villas, all decorated with tropical flair and most located in the Chocolate Hole/Great Cruz Bay area. A six-bedroom villa at Bordeaux called Captain's Quarters practically qualifies as a castle. ☏ 888-693-7676 • www.island-getaways.net

5 Vacation Homes, St. John

Managed by Kathy Demar and her small staff, Vacation Homes has a dozen top-of-the-line villas with fine sea views and tropical breezes; most of them are high in the hills along the north shore. The company is known for its attention to service, including stocking the refrigerator with milk and bread. ☏ 340-776-6094

6 Sea View Homes, St. John

Owned by Mark and Nanci Shekleton, Sea View Homes delivers just what it promises – luxury homes with sea views. All are in the Great Cruz Bay/Chocolate Hole, Rendezvous Bay, and Fish Bay areas. Sizes range from a cozy cottage to five bedrooms, all with attractive tropical furnishings. ☏ 888-625-2963 • www.seaviewhomes.com

7 Windspree Vacation Homes, St. John

This company handles a number of houses in the Coral Bay area. The Castle is particularly intriguing – built of stone, it features a tower for even better sea views than you get from the main house. ☏ 340-693-5423 • www.windspree.com

8 Calypso Realty, St. Thomas

While Calypso Realty's main business is selling houses, the company also has a half-dozen vacation villas, all with superb sea views and luxury furnishings. Most are located along St. Thomas's north shore, including two within the Mahogany Run community, next to the island's only golf course (see p77). ☏ 800-747-4858 • www.calypsorealty.com

9 McLaughlin Anderson Villas, USVI & BVI

The majority of this company's 150 villas are on St. Thomas, but there are also some good ones in St. Croix, St. John, Tortola, and Virgin Gorda, and two on Anegada. Most are top-end luxury homes, but you can find an occasional cottage. ☏ 800-537-6246 • www.mclaughlinanderson.com

10 Areana Villas, Tortola

A couple of this company's villas and apartments are on the beach, while some are located only a short walk or drive from lovely white sand, and others sit in the hills along the north shore. ☏ 284-494-5864 • www.areanavillas.com

Left **Buccaneer Hotel, St. Croix** Center **Grand Bay Palace, St. Thomas** Right **Biras Creek, VG**

Luxury Places to Stay

1 The Buccaneer Hotel, St. Croix

Spacious rooms sporting decorative touches, lovely views, and attentive staff make a stay here a luxury. This full-service resort offers an 18-hole golf course, several tennis courts, watersports, great dining, a fitness center, and a spa.
Ⓢ Map D4 • 800-255-3881 • www.thebuccaneer.com • $$$$ (incl breakfast)

2 Caneel Bay Resort, St. John

This exclusive hotel features seven beaches, lots of activities, fine restaurants, and a staff that stays on its toes. For the ultimate visit, opt for Cottage Seven, once the vacation spot of the resort's original owner Laurance Rockefeller.
Ⓢ Map D2 • 888-767-3966 • www.caneelbay.com • $$$$$ (incl breakfast)

3 Morning Star Beach Resort, St. Thomas

Part of the Marriott chain, Morning Star has it all – a great beachfront location, access to the amenities at adjacent Frenchman's Reef, and a superb restaurant. Ⓢ Map B2 • 800-228-9290 • www.marriott.com • $$$$

4 Grand Bay Palace Spa & Resort, St. Thomas

This hotel offers a comfortable stay with services and activities

such as a spa, a fitness center, watersports, tennis, and restaurants at the hotel (see Baywinds and Smugglers, p37) and nearby. The acclaimed Mahogany Run Golf Course is 3 miles (5 km) away. Ⓢ Map C2 • 800-322-2976 • www.palaceresorts.com • $$$

5 Ritz-Carlton, St. Thomas

The ritziest place to stay in St. Thomas, this hotel at Great Bay has staff that attends to every detail (including bringing a drink when you raise the flag on your beach chaise), luxurious rooms, and fabulous food at its dining rooms. Ⓢ Map D2 • 800-241-3333 • www.ritz-carlton.com • $$$$$

6 Biras Creek Hotel, Virgin Gorda

Luxury is understated at this remote hotel on the island's eastern side, with casual suites, showers open to the heavens, and transportation by bicycle. Gourmet fare at the gracious restaurant is the star attraction. Ⓢ Map M3 • 800-223-1108 • www.birascreek.com • $$$$$ (incl breakfast, lunch, afternoon tea & dinner)

7 Little Dix Bay, Virgin Gorda

Located on a crescent of white sand just outside Spanish Town, this resort combines tropical luxury with watersports activities. Its spa is one of the

best in this part of the Caribbean. Ⓢ Map L4 • 800-767-3966 • www.littledixbay.com • $$$$$ (incl breakfast)

8 Necker Island

Owned by British tycoon Richard Branson, the 74-acre Necker Island provides a posh retreat for upto 26 people in three houses. While away your days at the white beach, in the Jacuzzi, or playing a game of snooker. Ⓢ Map M3 • 800-557-4255 • www.neckerisland.com • $$$$$ (incl all meals & drinks)

9 Guana Island

A mere 30 guests share 850 acres at this remote retreat off Tortola's north coast. There are seven lovely beaches scattered around the island. Relax in secluded cottages with understated furnishings. Ⓢ Map J3 • 800-223-1108 • www.guanaislandbvi.com • $$$$$ (incl breakfast, lunch, afternoon tea & dinner)

10 Peter Island Resort & Yacht Club

Tropical elegance reigns at this resort with its colorful rooms. Tool around the bay on free kayaks and windsurfers, ride mountain bikes, and enjoy the splendid cuisine at the hotel's two restaurants. Ⓢ Map J5 • 800-346-4451 • www.peterisland.com • $$$$$ (incl breakfast, lunch, afternoon tea & dinner)

For more on some of these hotels **See pp26–7, 115**

Price Categories

For a standard, double room per night (with breakfast if included), taxes and extra charges.

$	under $100
$$	$100–200
$$$	$200–350
$$$$	$350–500
$$$$$	over $500

Left **Carringtons Inn, St. Croix** Right **Inn at Blackbeard's Castle, St. Thomas**

TOP 10 Small but Special Places to Stay

1 Carringtons Inn, St. Croix

Tucked away in the hills above Christiansted, this sophisticated B&B has five rooms with floral themes and private baths. *Map D5* • 877-658-0508 • www.carringtonsinn.com • *$$ (incl breakfast)*

2 Villa Margarita, St. Croix

Sitting seaside near Salt River, the casual Villa Margarita has suites with tropical decor, kitchens, lovely views, and the beach close by. Christiansted's shops are only a 15-minute drive away. *Map C4* • 866-274-8811 • www.villamargarita.com • *$$*

3 Concordia Eco-Tents, St. John

Part of the Maho Bay Camps *(see p115)* family, the Eco-Tents is very environmentally friendly – it uses solar energy for power and water conservation methods such as waterless toilets. Snorkeling, swimming, and hiking at Salt Pond Bay are just a five-minute drive away. *Map F2* • 800-392-9004 • www.maho.org • *$$*

4 Garden by the Sea, St. John

This cozy B&B provides casual accommodation located an easy walk from Cruz Bay's shops. A pocket beach at nearby Frank Bay beckons. The small rooms come with nice touches such as mosquito nets. *Map D2* • 340-779-4731 • www.gardenbythesea.com • *$$$ (incl breakfast)*

5 Inn at Blackbeard's Castle, St. Thomas

Fabulous harbor and city views greet you from the terrace and many rooms at this cozy hotel sitting high up above Charlotte Amalie. Several rooms have four-poster beds. Island lore has it that the hotel's 17th-century stone tower was used as a lookout by the pirate Blackbeard. *Map P1* • 800-344-5771 • www.blackbeardscastle.com • *$$ (incl breakfast)*

6 Frenchman's Cay Hotel, Tortola

Fronting the water at Frenchman's Cay and within walking distance of Soper's Hole Marina and West End, this hotel has nine condominiums, mostly in neutral tones. Spend your days at the small pool, the man-made beach, or snorkeling and kayaking the waters of Drake's Passage. *Map G5* • 800-235-4077 • www.frenchmans.com • *$$$*

7 Myett's Garden Inn, Tortola

Located just steps from Cane Garden Bay beach on the island's north side, this small hotel has rooms with a fresh, tropical feel. Apart from the hotel's Garden Grille, there are several dining and nightlife options in Cane Garden Bay. *Map G4* • 284-495-9649 • www.myettent.com • *$$*

8 Sugar Mill Hotel, Tortola

With an old sugar mill as its centerpiece, this hotel has 24 rooms, suites, and a villa scattered up the hillside at Apple Bay. Its restaurant is a big draw *(see p31 & p85)*. Rooms are done in tropical brights and pastels, and there's a small beach and a pool. *Map G4* • 800-462-8834 • www.sugarmillhotel.com • *$$$*

9 Sandy Ground Estates, Jost Van Dyke

The place to go if you want to get away from it all, this resort has eight villas above a stretch of white sandy beach where you can read to your heart's content, socialize at the beach, or simply enjoy the quiet. *Map H3* • 284-494-3391 • www.sandyground.com • *$$$ per day for a week's stay*

10 Cooper Island Beach Club

A casual beachfront place just right for relaxation, the hotel has a barefoot ambience, a style that is fast disappearing in the Caribbean. Cook meals in the kitchenettes attached to all rooms, or enjoy the camaraderie at the two small restaurants. *Map K5* • 800-542-4624 • www.cooper-island.com • *$$$*

Left **Cane Bay, St. Croix** Right **Leverick Bay Resort Hotel, Virgin Gorda**

TOP 10 Casual Places to Stay

1 Divi Carina Bay Resort & Casino, St. Croix
Rooms done in blue and white with kitchenettes stretch along the beach at Turner Hole. The casino (see p36) is a major draw and the resort's Starlight Bar & Grille offers excellent dining. ✆ Map F4 • 877-773-9700 • www. divicarina.com • $$$

2 Hibiscus Beach Resort, St. Croix
The hotel's 38 rooms snuggle up to a white sandy beach on the island's north shore at La Grande Princesse. Rooms are modern with patios or balconies, floral accents, and great sea views. Christiansted's dining and shopping sit just a 10-minute drive away. ✆ Map C4 • 800-442-0121 • www.1hibiscus.com • $$ (incl breakfast)

3 Tamarind Reef Hotel, St. Croix
Buck Island and Green Cay on the island's north shore dot your view at this small motel at the water's edge; each room has a patio or balcony. The beach is on the rocky side, but the snorkeling is excellent. ✆ Map E4 • 800-619-0014 • www. usvi.net/ hotel/tamarind • $$$ (incl breakfast)

4 Waves at Cane Bay, St. Croix
Dive just off the beach at this 12-room resort sitting seaside near Cane Bay's Wall. Indeed, if you're a certified diver, dive and snorkel gear are included in your room rate. Rooms have tropical decor, patios or balconies, kitchens or kitchenettes, and gorgeous sea views. ✆ Map B4 • 800-545-0603 • www. canebaystcroix.com • $$

5 Estate Zootenvaal, St. John
Get away from the crowd at this cottage colony on protected Hurricane Hole. The three units, all with kitchens, are near the water or across the road from the private beach. Superb snorkeling. ✆ Map F2 • 340-776-6321 • www.usviguide.com/zootenvaal • $$$

6 Best Western, Emerald Beach, St. Thomas
A glorious strand of pristine beach on the island's southwest shore is minutes from your doorstep at this small resort with tropical modern rooms, a restaurant, and watersports. A complimentary shuttle runs to the Charlotte Amalie shopping district. ✆ Map B2 • 800-233-4936 • www.emeraldbeach.com • $$$ (incl breakfast)

7 Sebastian's on the Beach, Tortola
With beachfront and garden rooms, this spot at Apple Bay conjures up images of the old Caribbean. In spite of the modern touches in the rooms, there's something in the air that takes you back decades. ✆ Map G4 • 800-336-4870 • www. sebastiansbvi.com • $$

8 Leverick Bay Resort, Virgin Gorda
Starting with the gaily painted buildings, this resort exudes energy – most guests get busy with day sails, scuba trips, or power boat rentals. Rooms, decorated in tropical style, have grand sea views. ✆ Map M3 • 800-848-7081 • www. leverickbay.com • $$

9 Neptune's Treasure, Anegada
A stay at this hotel, next to a stunning beach on the island's southwest side, guarantees relaxation. There isn't much else to do – you can snorkel, take a taxi ride to see the island's flamingos, or go fishing. ✆ Map K1 • 284-495-9439 • www. neptunestreasure.com • $$

10 Sandcastle, Jost Van Dyke
Spend your days in the hammock in the sandy beach at White Bay, snorkeling in the clear waters, hiking over to Great Bay, or socializing with other guests at this casual spot. There are only six units (including two on the beach), so you won't feel crowded. ✆ Map G3 • 284-495-9888 • www. sandcastle-bvi.com • $$$

Breakfasts in all hotels vary from a roll and juice to hearty fare

Price Categories

For a standard, double room per night (with breakfast if included), taxes and extra charges.

$	under $100
$$	$100–200
$$$	$200–350
$$$$	$350–500
$$$$$	over $500

Left **Beach at Westin Resort, St. John** Right **Child's Grove, Little Dix Bay, Virgin Gorda**

🔟 Good Family Places to Stay

1 The Buccaneer Hotel, St. Croix

With a free year-round kids' camp for 4–12 year-olds, the Buccaneer makes a fine family destination. Running from 9:30am to 5:30pm, the camp has your kids swimming, making arts and crafts, and listening to stories. Children stay free in the same room as adults. The summer packages are often family-oriented *(see p112)*.

2 Chenay Bay Beach Resort, St. Croix

Facilities at this resort in Green Cay include kitchenettes and connecting rooms or rollaway beds for kids, who stay free in their parents' room. The Cruzan Kid's program includes snorkeling and kayaking lessons and hiking. 🅢 *Map E4 • 800-548-4457 • www.chenaybay.com • $$$*

3 Cinnamon Bay Campground, St. John

There's no kids' program at this beachfront Virgin Islands National Park campground, but your kids will find lots of other children to play with. There's a good restaurant *(see also p119).* 🅢 *Map E2 • 800-539-9998 • www.cinnamonbay.com • $$*

4 Westin Resort & Villas, St. John

Sitting beachfront at Great Cruz Bay, the Westin Resort has a

kids' club. Families are attracted in summer by package plans. Kids like the pool, where they get to mix with their peers. 🅢 *Map D2 • 800-808-5020 • www.westinresortstjohn.com • $$$$$*

5 Caneel Bay Resort, St. John

Located in Virgin Islands National Park, this resort has a kids' club that gives children an appreciation for the island's environment and the resort. Kids do arts and crafts and dig in tide pools while their parents relax *(see p112)*.

6 Maho Bay Camps, St. John

Canvas cottages open to the breezes and a kids' arts and crafts program make this camp popular with families. The small beach and terrific snorkeling keep children busy for hours. A casual dining room serves meals, giving the family chef a break from the propane stove *(see also p119)*. 🅢 *Map E2 • 800-392-9004 • www.maho.org • $$*

7 Bolongo Bay Beach Club, St. Thomas

The myriad activities at Bolongo Bay will keep even the most active child busy. And since kids under 12 stay free in their parents' room, you'll have some money left for extras. Summer packages often include

free children's meals, while guests opting for the all- and semi-inclusive plans get complimentary watersports gear. 🅢 *Map C2 • 800-524-4746 • www.bolongobay.com • $$$ (incl breakfast)*

8 Grand Bay Palace Spa & Resort, St. Thomas

With a beachfront location and a kids' club, the resort attracts lots of families, particularly at Christmas and in summer. Popular Coral World is only half a mile (1 km) away *(see p112)*.

9 Wyndham Sugar Bay Resort & Spa, St. Thomas

This Smith Bay resort's all-inclusive plan makes it a good deal for families, who won't have to spend extra for non-motorized watersports toys and dining at several restaurants. The kids' club is free and rooms have ample space for children and parents. 🅢 *Map C2 • 877-999-3223 • www.wyndham.com • $$$$$*

10 Little Dix Bay, Virgin Gorda

Kids play dress up and do arts and crafts at the Child's Grove, giving parents a break. There's a complimentary party for children during the Monday manager's sunset cocktail party. A long sandy beach and lots of watersports make this a good bet *(see p112)*.

Where they are not free, kids' camps and clubs are priced on a per day basis in most hotels

Left **Village Cay Hotel, Tortola** Right **Bitter End Yacht Club, Virgin Gorda**

Nautical Places to Stay

1 Anchorage Condominiums, St. Thomas

Come spring, this spot in Estate Nazareth gets busy when sailors gather next door at the St. Thomas Yacht Club for the annual Rolex Regatta. Meet yachties at the beach, rent power boats, or take a day sail from Red Hook, a short drive away. ⊗ *Map C2 • 800-874-7897 • www.antillesresorts.com • $$$$*

2 Hodge's Creek Marina, Tortola

This 23-room hotel, on the island's eastern side, is at the sheltered Hodge's Creek, center of the Sunsail Charter marine scene. Meet old salts at the hotel's bar, or spend your days gazing out to sea from your airy hotel room. ⊗ *Map J4 • 284-494-5000 • www.hodgescreek.com • $$$*

3 Nanny Cay Marina, Tortola

A boat yard and busy marina serve as the heart of this south shore spot. Rent power boats, hop into a day sail boat for a trip around Drake's Passage, or stay ashore to enjoy meals at the two restaurants. ⊗ *Map H5 • 866-284-4683 • www.nannycay.com • $$*

4 Moorings-Mariner Inn, Tortola

The marina at Wickhams Cay II houses bare and crewed boats (see p22)

aplenty. Guests heading out for a trip often stay ashore at night, socializing at the marina's bar with sailors working on their boats at the adjacent boat yard. ⊗ *Map H4 • 800-535-7289 • www.moorings.com • $$*

5 Prospect Reef Resort, Tortola

Prospect Reef's Learn to Sail packages couple accommodations with sailing lessons. For the less nautically inclined, this full-service resort has plenty of land activities including tennis and high tea. ⊗ *Map H4 • 800-356-8937 • www.prospectreef.com • $$*

6 Village Cay Hotel & Marina, Tortola

Located in the heart of Road Town and at one of the island's busiest marinas, this 21-room hotel gives visitors a nautical scene with shopping and many restaurants nearby. Rooms, all with fresh tropical accents, overlook either the sea or the pool. ⊗ *Map H4 • 284-494-2771 • www.villagecay.com • $$*

7 Pusser's, Marina Cay

Just a short hop off Tortola's north shore on its own island, Pusser's is a favorite sailboat anchorage. The bar brings in sailors of all hues for Pusser's Painkillers, a frothy rum concoction (see also p35). Rooms, all

with stellar sea views and balconies, have windows open to the trade winds. ⊗ *Map J4 • 888-873-5226 • www.pussers.com • $$$*

8 Bitter End Yacht Club, Virgin Gorda

It's hard to get more nautical than this place in North Sound, accessible only by ferry and surrounded by boats of all sizes. Guests can learn the ropes at the hotel's acclaimed sailing school (see p92). ⊗ *Map M3 • 800-872-2392 • www.beyc.com • $$$$$ (incl breakfast, lunch & dinner)*

9 Saba Rock Resort, Virgin Gorda

Saba Rock, a mere speck reached only by boat, has special rates for boaters who need a break from the nautical life. Those without a private yacht are picked up by ferry. Nice bar and restaurant. ⊗ *Map M3 • 284-495-7711 • www.sabarock.com • $$*

10 Anegada Reef Hotel

This hotel off the beaten path lures boaters for a few hours at its casual bar or restaurant (see p93). Landlubbers like the rooms' tropical style and the spectacular snorkeling right off the hotel's stunning white beach. ⊗ *Map K1 • 284-495-8002 • www.anegadareef.com • $$$ (incl breakfast, lunch & dinner)*

Price Categories

For a standard, double room per night (with breakfast if included), taxes, and extra charges.

$	under $100
$$	$100–200
$$$	$200–350
$$$$	$350–500
$$$$$	over $500

Left **Sugar Beach Resort, St. Croix** Right **Gallows Point Resort, St. John**

Condominiums

1 Sugar Beach Resort, St. Croix

Located on a stretch of powdery white sand just outside Christiansted, this resort has units ranging from studios to four bedrooms, all with fresh breezes and glorious views. Have a dip in the pool, built around an old sugar mill. ✣ Map D4 • 800-524-2049 • www.sugarbeachstcroix. com • $$$

2 Villa Madeline, St. Croix

Sitting hillside above Teague Bay, the units at Villa Madeline provide the ultimate in privacy, with each having its own pool. The restaurant draws both visitors and residents. A golf course is nearby. ✣ Map E4 • 800-237-1959 • www.teaguebayproperties. com • $$$ per day for a week's stay

3 Coconut Coast Villas, St. John

Located at Turner Bay, only a 10-minute walk from Cruz Bay's shops and restaurants, Coconut Coast offers units in various sizes, with balconies, tropical furnishings, and original art on the walls. The beach is rocky, but the snorkeling is superb. ✣ Map D2 • 800-858-7989 • www. coconutcoast.com • $$$

4 Concordia Studios, St. John

Part of the appeal of this place is its location way out on the island's southeast edge. Salt Pond Bay, with its excellent snorkeling and hiking, is a short drive away. ✣ Map F2 • 800-392-9004 • www.maho.org • $$

5 Gallows Point Resort, St. John

Overlooking Cruz Bay harbor, this 60-unit complex is a few minutes walk from Cruz Bay's conveniences. The one-bedroom suites have a fresh tropical flair and magnificent sea views. Its Zozo's Ristorante (see p69) draws crowds. ✣ Map D2 • 800-323-7229 • www.gallowspointresort. com • $$$$

6 Sapphire Beach Resort, St. Thomas

Suites at this resort in Smith Bay overlook the ocean or the marina; all have decks or balconies. Watersports reign here, with snorkeling gear, Sunfish sailboats, and floats all complimentary. ✣ Map C2 • 800-524-2029 • www. sapphirebeach.com • $$$$

7 Secret Harbour Beach Resort, St. Thomas

Studio and one- and two-bedroom units in Estate Nazareth front onto an attractive crescent of white sand perfect for sunning. All units have patios or decks, and attractive tropical furnishings. The café (see p79) is definitely worth a stop. This is one of the few disabled access resorts. ✣ Map C2 • 800-524-2250 • www.secretharbourvi. com • $$$

8 Lighthouse Villas, Tortola

Located in Cane Garden Bay village, this small complex has units with lots of windows and balconies to enjoy the view. Cane Bay can be a lively place, with the bars and restaurants going full tilt on some nights. A sandy beach sits just across the road. ✣ Map G4 • 284-494-5482 • www.travel-watch. com/lighthouse • $$ per day for a week's stay

9 Long Bay Beach Resort, Tortola

Scattered up the hill above Long Bay on the island's west side, this resort's units provide great views and all the amenities of a full-service resort. Swim at the pool, dine at the restaurants, and sunbathe at the sandy beach. ✣ Map G5 • 877-913-2525 • www. longbay.com • $$$

10 Nail Bay Resort, Virgin Gorda

Stretching up the hill above three lovely beaches, Nail Bay's spacious condominium units span a range of sizes from rooms to suites to apartments to large villas. There's a free-form pool with a swim-up bar. ✣ Map L3 • 800-871-3551 • www. nailbayresort.com • $$

Left **King Christian, St. Croix** Center **Pink Fancy, St. Croix** Right **Fischer's Cove, Virgin Gorda**

In-town Places to Stay

1 King Christian Hotel, St. Croix

Sitting on the waterfront at Christiansted, this hotel has rooms with balconies ideal for watching boats in the harbor; less expensive rooms have city views. Head for the town or beach, or stick around to enjoy the courtyard pool. ✪ Map D4 • 340-773-6339 • www. kingchristian.com • $$

2 Pink Fancy Hotel, St. Croix

Antiques, oriental rugs, and other nice touches fill the rooms at this historic hotel on downtown Christiansted's fringes. Each of the 13 rooms is different, but all have kitchenettes. ✪ Map D5 • 800-524-2045 • www. pinkfancy.com • $$ (incl breakfast in some rooms)

3 Inn at Tamarind Court, St. John

This rambling spot features a popular courtyard restaurant. The 22 rooms are fresh with tropical colors; six of them share baths. Not much of a view, but the convenience of being close to Cruz Bay's shopping and dining lures visitors. ✪ Map D2 • 800-221-1637 • www.stjohninn. com/tamarindcourt • $$ (incl breakfast)

4 St. John Inn

With names that reflect the owners' California roots, the 13 rooms at this small hotel at Cruz Bay's edge have different sizes and decor. Guests gather at the small pool or the hotel bar after a shopping or beach trip. ✪ Map D2 • 800-666-7688 • www. stjohninn.com • $$

5 Crystal Palace, St. Thomas

Once the home of a well-known St. Thomas family, this hotel situated on Charlotte Amalie's Crystal Gade is filled with family heirlooms. Rooms are different sizes; only a few have private baths. A stay here puts you close to shopping, restaurants, and historic district sights. ✪ Map N2 • 866-502-2277 • www.crystalpalaceusvi. com • $$ (incl breakfast)

6 Holiday Inn, Windward Passage, St. Thomas

This mid-rise hotel across the road from the Charlotte Amalie waterfront attracts business people and vacationers who want a modern, in-town location. Rooms have typical Holiday Inn amenities, but sport tropical touches. Take a taxi to the beach or linger at the pool. ✪ Map B2 • 800-524-7389 • www.holidayinn.st-thomas.com • $$$

7 Hotel 1829, St. Thomas

Finished in 1829, the building was the home of a French sea captain; its 15 rooms have an old-world charm with modern touches. The location, on a hill overlooking Charlotte Amalie Harbor and the city, places it in the heart of the shopping and restaurant district. ✪ Map P2 • 800-524-2002 • www.hotel1829.com • $$ (incl breakfast)

8 Maria's Hotel by the Sea, Tortola

Bright colors complement white walls at this hotel, minutes by foot from Road Town's shopping, restaurants, and nightlife. The beach is a 15-minute drive away. ✪ Map H4 • 284-494-2595 • www. mariasbythesea.com • $$

9 Treasure Isle Hotel, Tortola

Located near Wickhams Cay II in Road Town, this hotel puts you within walking distance of shops and restaurants. Relax by the pool, go sailing, or take the hotel shuttle to its restaurant at Cane Garden Bay. ✪ Map H4 • 284-494-2501 • www.treasureislehotel. net • $$

10 Fischer's Cove Beach Hotel, Virgin Gorda

Stroll from your room onto the beach at this casual spot in Spanish Town. Some rooms front on the beach; others are tucked back in the garden. The restaurant is excellent. ✪ Map L4 • 284-495-5252 • www. fischerscove.com • $$

Price Categories

For a standard, double room per night (with breakfast if included), taxes, and extra charges.	**$** under $100
	$$ $100–200
	$$$ $200–350
	$$$$ $350–500
	$$$$$ over $500

Left **Breakfast Club, St. Croix** Right **Maho Bay Camps, St. John**

₀10 Budget Places to Stay

1 Breakfast Club, St. Croix

Within walking distance of downtown Christiansted, this hotel has bright, modest rooms, all with kitchens. Breakfast on delicious banana pancakes, then linger in the hammock or head out to beaches or the town's historic sights and shops. ◈ Map D5 • 340-773-7383 • http://nav.to/thebreakfastclub • $ (incl breakfast)

2 Cinnamon Bay Campground, St. John

Located in the Virgin Islands National Park, this campground has shady and secluded sites for pitching tents. You can also rent erected tents and cottages. Amenities such as a restaurant and watersports rentals make this almost a resort (see p115).

3 Maho Bay Camps, St. John – Work Exchange Program

Stay free for a month or more in a tent at the environmentally friendly Maho Bay Camps if you don't mind working four hours a day doing jobs such as cooking, carpentry, and maintenance. Apply online only (see p115).

4 VI Environmental Resource Station, St. John – Work Exchange Program

Work four hours a day at a research station in remote Lameshur Bay. In exchange for doing various jobs, you get a bed, all meals, and a chance to spend time at a glorious beach and enjoy the place's camaraderie. ◈ Map E2 • 888-647-2501 • www.islands.org/virgin/viers

5 Danish Chalet Inn, St. Thomas

Sitting in the hills above Charlotte Amalie, the Danish Chalet has modest accommodations in a friendly atmosphere. Guests tend to be convivial, gathering on the veranda for breakfast. You can use the pool at the hotel across the street. ◈ Map B2 • 877-407-2567 • www.danishchaletinn.com • $ (incl breakfast)

6 Island View Guest House, St. Thomas

The hillside Island View Guest House, northwest of Charlotte Amalie, delivers just that – a gorgeous view of St. Thomas from its spacious porch. Rooms are homey with a tropical touch. Enjoy a swim in the pool, or head out for the beach, to take in the sights or shop in nearby Charlotte Amalie. ◈ Map B2 • 800-524-2023 • www.st-thomas.com/islandviewguesthouse • $ (incl breakfast)

7 Brewers Bay Campground, Tortola

Take the winding Brewers Bay East Road to this very casual campground. Rented tents are on the ramshackle side (best to bring your own). Bar and restaurant with fun atmosphere. ◈ Map H4 • 284-494-3463 • $

8 Hotel Castle Maria, Tortola

Located just outside Road Town, this has slightly dowdy rooms, all with balconies and some with full kitchens. Make it the base for a busy Tortola vacation, returning for a swim in the pool or dinner at restaurant. ◈ Map H4 • 284-494-2553 • www.islandsonline.com/hotelcastlemaria • $

9 Jolly Roger Inn, Tortola

Clean, basic rooms in knock-your-socks-off colors such as purple and blue and a good restaurant; some rooms have shared baths. A stay here puts you near Soper's Hole's shopping and just a minute from the West End ferry. ◈ Map G5 • 284-495-4559 • www.jollyrogerbvi.com • $

10 White Bay Campground, Jost Van Dyke

Stay in a tent or rent a cabin at this modest spot. You can snorkel the clear White Bay waters, hike around the island, or hang out at the gorgeous beach or the bar. There might be music – peace is not guaranteed. ◈ Map G3 • 284-495-9358 • $

For the Work Exchange Program at VI Environmental Resource Station at St. John, apply via e-mail at viers@islands.org

General Index

Index

Index

Index

Acknowledgements

The Author
Long time St. John resident Lynda Lohr lives in Coral Bay. A reporter by trade, she has written for numerous national, regional, and local publications as well as travel websites. On her rare days off, she swims at Great Maho Bay and hikes the island's numerous trails.

Photographer Linda Whitwam

Additional Photography
Jane Burton, Colin Keates, Geoff Brightling, Deni Bown

DK INDIA

Managing Editor
Aruna Ghose

Art Editor
Benu Joshi

Project Editor
Rimli Borooah

Project Designer
Pallavi Narain

Senior Cartographer
Uma Bhattacharya

Cartographer
Alok Pathak

Picture Researcher
Taiyaba Khatoon

DTP Co-ordinator
Shailesh Sharma

DTP Designer
Vinod Harish

Fact-checker
Lynda Lohr

Indexer
Shreya Arora

DK LONDON

Publisher
Douglas Amrine

Publishing Manager
Anna Streiffert

Managing Art Editor
Jane Ewart

Senior Cartographic Editor
Casper Morris

Senior DTP Designer
Jason Little

Production
Melanie Dowland

Picture Credits
t-top; tl-top left; tr-top right; tfr-top far right; c-center; cl-center left; cla-center left above; clb-center left below; cra-center right above; crb-center right below; b-bottom; bl-bottom left; bc-bottom center; br-bottom right; bfr-bottom far right.

Every effort has been made to trace the copyright holders,

Acknowledgements

and we apologize in advance for any unintentional omissions. We would be pleased to insert the appropriate acknowledgements in any subsequent edition of this publication.

The publishers would like to thank the following individuals, companies and picture libraries for their kind permission to reproduce their photographs.

CORBIS: 20bl; Bettmann 48tl, 49bfr; Jonathan Blair 21crb; Duomo 49tfr; Macduff Everton 110t; Wolfgang Kaehler 14–15; Catherine Karnow 22tr; Bob Krist 3br; Conroy Michael/ Corbis Sygma 49bl; Neil Rabinowitz 54–5;

Courtesy of BIRAS CREEK RESORT, VIRGIN GORDA 7crb, 26-27, 51tfr, 103tr, 112tr;

Courtesy of THE DANISH NATIONAL ARCHIVES "The Danish West Indian government in St. Croix, no. 81.577" 48bl;

Courtesy of SUGAR MILL RESTAURANT, TORTOLA 30tr;

DON HEBERT: 4–5, 18cla, 22 bc, 50tl, 63b, 77bc, 90b, 104t;

REUTERS: 98t;

STEVE SIMONSEN / MARINE SCENES: 6clb, 7cra, 10–11, 12–13, 19bl, 24cla, 24–5, 24bc, 25tl, 25cra, 25crb, 27bc, 28–9, 36tl, 37tfr, 39t, 39cl, 44tl, 44tr, 44br, 46tl, 46tr, 46bc, 47tfr, 47bfr, 50b, 66tl, 66tr, 86–7, 94–5, 96tl, 107tl.

FRONT COVER: ALAMY: Stephen Frink Collection/ William Harrington b; CORBIS: Royalty-Free ca; DK Picture Library: t; ROBERT HARDING: Royalty-Free main image cb.

BACK COVER: CORBIS: Macduff Everton l; Royalty-Free c, r.

All other images are © Dorling Kindersley. For further information see: www.dkimages.com.

Dorling Kindersley Special Editions

Dorling Kindersley books can be purchased in bulk quantities at discounted prices for use in promotions or as premiums. We are also able to offer special editions and personalized jackets, corporate imprints, and excerpts from all of our books, tailored specifically to meet your own needs.

To find out more, please contact: (in the United Kingdom) – Sarah.Burgess@dk.com or Special Sales, Dorling Kindersley Limited, 80 Strand, London WC2R 0RL; (in the United States) – Special Markets Department, DK Publishing, Inc., 375 Hudson Street, New York, New York 10014.